The Govern

# Governance of Regulators' Practices

ACCOUNTABILITY, TRANSPARENCY
AND CO-ORDINATION

This work is published under the responsibility of the Secretary-General of the OECD. The opinions expressed and arguments employed herein do not necessarily reflect the official views of OECD member countries.

This document and any map included herein are without prejudice to the status of or sovereignty over any territory, to the delimitation of international frontiers and boundaries and to the name of any territory, city or area.

**Please cite this publication as:**
OECD (2016), *Governance of Regulators' Practices: Accountability, Transparency and Co-ordination*, The Governance of Regulators, OECD Publishing, Paris.
http://dx.doi.org/10.1787/9789264255388-en

ISBN 978-92-64-25537-1 (print)
ISBN 978-92-64-25538-8 (PDF)

Series: The Governance of Regulators
ISSN 2415-1432 (print)
ISSN 2415-1440 (online)

The statistical data for Israel are supplied by and under the responsibility of the relevant Israeli authorities. The use of such data by the OECD is without prejudice to the status of the Golan Heights, East Jerusalem and Israeli settlements in the West Bank under the terms of international law.

**Photo credits:** Cover © Leigh Prather - Fotolia.com.

Corrigenda to OECD publications may be found on line at: *www.oecd.org/about/publishing/corrigenda.htm*.

© OECD 2016

You can copy, download or print OECD content for your own use, and you can include excerpts from OECD publications, databases and multimedia products in your own documents, presentations, blogs, websites and teaching materials, provided that suitable acknowledgement of OECD as source and copyright owner is given. All requests for public or commercial use and translation rights should be submitted to *rights@oecd.org*. Requests for permission to photocopy portions of this material for public or commercial use shall be addressed directly to the Copyright Clearance Center (CCC) at *info@copyright.com* or the Centre français d'exploitation du droit de copie (CFC) at *contact@cfcopies.com*.

# Foreword

Economic regulators help ensure access to and quality of public utilities, facilitate infrastructure investment and protect market neutrality. They play a crucial role in supporting sustainable and inclusive growth and trust in public institutions. The role of the regulator, how it co-ordinates with other public institutions, the powers it is given and how it is held accountable for exercising these powers together form a "governance architecture." This architecture needs to be well crafted and appropriately implemented, if the regulator is to succeed in combining effective regulation with a high level of trust.

This report looks at the way in which four regulators -- the Australian Competition & Consumer Commission (ACCC), the Australian Energy Regulator (AER), Portugal's Water and Waste Services Regulation Authority (ERSAR), and the UK Office of Rail and Road (ORR) -- have addressed these governance challenges. The report finds that clarity and transparency on what is expected from regulators and what regulators can do to meet these expectations are crucial. Clarity on the respective roles of ministries, other government agencies and regulators can also help avoid institutional and co-ordination gaps. Regulators can proactively contribute to clarity and good co-ordination through clear and comprehensive annual reports, targeted, accessible and assessable information, transparent advice to government and parliament and fit-for-purpose co-ordination mechanisms that are adapted to the objectives to be achieved. Management commitment is also essential to ensure the cultural acceptance of accountability and transparency throughout the organisation and make co-ordination arrangements work in practice.

This report contributes to the OECD work programme on the governance of regulators and regulatory policy led by the OECD Network of Economic Regulators and the OECD Regulatory Policy Committee with the support of the Regulatory Policy Division of the OECD Public Governance and Territorial Development Directorate. The Directorate's mission is to help government at all levels design and implement strategic, evidence-based and innovative policies to strengthen public governance, respond effectively to diverse and disruptive economic, social and environmental challenges and deliver on government's commitments to citizens. The goal is to support countries in building better government systems and implementing policies at both national and regional level that lead to sustainable economic and social development.

This work was undertaken with the support of the Federal Government of Mexico, which is interested in identifying good practices that can inform and underpin the implementation of its reforms of regulatory agencies.

## Acknowledgements

The work underlying this report was led by Manuel Flores Romero and prepared by Filippo Cavassini with the encouragement and support of Rolf Alter, Director, Public Governance and Territorial Development Directorate, and Nick Malyshev, Head, Regulatory Policy Division, Public Governance and Territorial Development Directorate. Faisal Naru provided strategic advice in the development of the report. Jacobo Garcia Villareal co-ordinated the preparation of the case studies of the Australian Competition and Consumer Commission (ACCC), the Australian Energy Regulator (AER), Portugal's Water and Waste Services Regulation Authority (ERSAR) and the UK Office of Rail and Road (ORR) that helped inform the analysis. Céline Kauffmann provided inputs during the preparation of the case studies and the report. Guillermo Morales provided research assistance. Jennifer Stein co-ordinated the editorial process.

The report would have not been possible without the support of the Ministry of Finance of the Federal Government of Mexico and the OECD Network of Economic Regulators and those members that were instrumental in developing the case studies. Mark Pearson, former Chief Risk Officer, ACCC, took responsibility for the preparation of the three case studies. Substantive inputs for the preparation of the ORR and ERSAR case studies were provided by Daniel Brown, Director, Strategy and Policy, ORR, and David Alves, Head of the Strategic Projects Department, ERSAR. The report also benefitted from substantive inputs from Cristina Cifuentes, Commissioner, and Simon Haslock, Assistant Director, Regulatory Reform and Performance, ACCC, John Holmes, Head of Better Regulation and Policy, ORR, Daniel Curtis, Adviser, Regulatory Reform Division, Department of the Prime Minister and Cabinet, Australian Government.

The report was submitted to the OECD Network of Economic Regulators and to the OECD Regulatory Policy Committee for final comments in February 2016.

# Table of contents

Acronyms and abbreviations ............................................................................................. 9

Executive summary .......................................................................................................... 11

*Chapter 1.* The governance of regulators: overview and trends ................................ 15
    Overview ...................................................................................................................... 16
    Global trends ................................................................................................................ 17
    Notes ............................................................................................................................. 21
    Bibliography ................................................................................................................. 22

*Chapter 2.* Regulators' practices .................................................................................... 23
    Comparability across regulators .................................................................................. 25
    Accountability and transparency .................................................................................. 27
    Co-ordination ................................................................................................................ 39
    Guiding lessons ............................................................................................................ 44
    Notes ............................................................................................................................. 46
    Bibliography ................................................................................................................. 48

*Chapter 3.* Australian Energy Regulator and Australian Competition
& Consumer Commission's Telecommunications Regulation .................................... 49
    Section A: ACCC and AER organisational frameworks ............................................ 50
    Reform agenda: Commonwealth governance measures .............................................. 54
    Accountability and transparency: ACCC and AER frameworks ................................ 56
    Section B: ACCC telecommunications regulatory framework ................................... 60
    Functions and powers .................................................................................................. 62
    Accountability to a minister and the legislature .......................................................... 64
    Accountability to regulated entities .............................................................................. 65
    Accountability to the public ......................................................................................... 66
    Transparency ................................................................................................................ 67
    Section C: AER regulatory framework ........................................................................ 68
    Notes ............................................................................................................................. 77
    Bibliography ................................................................................................................. 78

*Chapter 4.* **Portugal's Water and Waste Services Regulation Authority** ............ 79

Institutional setting ............................................................................................ 81
Mandate and role ................................................................................................ 85
Internal organisation .......................................................................................... 90
Accountability mechanisms ................................................................................ 92
Inter-institutional co-ordination and collaboration ............................................ 92
Concluding insights .......................................................................................... 102
Bibliography ..................................................................................................... 104

*Chapitre 5.* **The UK Office of Rail and Road (ORR)** ........................................ 105

Regulatory framework, objectives and functions ............................................. 106
Accountability and transparency ...................................................................... 124
Transparency .................................................................................................... 130
Concluding insights .......................................................................................... 132
Notes ................................................................................................................. 133
Bibliography ..................................................................................................... 135

*Chapter 6.* **Mexico's key sector and regulatory reforms** ................................... 137

Energy .............................................................................................................. 138
Telecommunications ......................................................................................... 140
Economic competition ...................................................................................... 141
Bibliography ..................................................................................................... 142

## Tables

1.1. Correlating independence, accountability and scope of action ................. 18
2.1. Mapping co-ordination stages, objectives and instruments ...................... 43
4.1. Indicators of water access and quality ...................................................... 82

## Figures

1.1. The OECD Best Practice Principles on the Governance of Regulators ..... 17
1.2. Regulators' scope of action ....................................................................... 19
1.3. Water regulators: legislative requirements for co-ordination .................... 20
1.4. Water regulators: co-ordination practices ................................................. 20
2.1. The governance of regulators in Australia, Mexico, Portugal
     and the United Kingdom .......................................................................... 26
2.2. Tracking industry performance at ORR .................................................... 36
2.3. Institutional arrangements for water regulation in Portugal ..................... 41
6.1. Energy regulatory framework in Mexico ................................................ 139

## Acronyms and abbreviations

| | |
|---|---|
| ACCC | Australian Competition & Consumer Commission |
| AER | Australian Energy Regulator |
| ANAO | Australian National Audit Office |
| APA | Portugal's Environmental Protection Agency |
| ASEA | Agency of Industrial Safety and Environmental Protection in the Oil and Gas Sector (*Mexico*) |
| CENACE | National Energy Control Centre (*Mexico*) |
| CENAGAS | National Centre for Control of Natural Gas (*Mexico*) |
| CEO | Chief Executive Office |
| CNIH | National Centre for Hydrocarbon Information (*Mexico*) |
| COAG | Council of Australian Governments |
| CRE | Energy Regulation Commission (*Mexico*) |
| EC | Executive Committee |
| ERSAR | Portugal's Water and Waste Services Regulation Authority |
| HFC | hybrid fibre coaxial |
| HSE | Health and Safety Executive |
| IRAR | Institute for Regulation of Water and Solid Waste |
| MOATE | Ministry for Environment and Energy |
| MoUs | Memoranda of Understanding |
| NAO | National Audit Office |
| ORR | Office of Rail and Road |
| PBS | Portfolio Budget Statement |
| PMR | Product Market Regulation |
| RPF | Regulator Performance Framework |
| SAI | Supreme Audit Institution |
| SoE | Statement of Expectations |
| SoI | Statement of Intent |

# Executive summary

Accountability and transparency are translated into practice through formal and informal measures. Formal accountability is fundamental, as regulatory agencies have significant powers, and their decisions affect investment decisions, property rights, financial returns, fees and charges paid by users. Accountability usually begins with the requirements that are embedded in the legislative structure of the regulatory regime:

- *Accountability to Parliament*, as provided in enabling legislation, may include specific parliamentary or governmental committees that oversee the financial probity and practices of the regulator, including through the publication of agency budgets in budget statements.

- *Legally binding requirements to adhere to proper standards of accounting and compliance with independent auditing*, often undertaken by the national audit body, include the publication of annual reports and judicial review of regulators' decisions.

There are other safeguards or measures that may be put in place to ensure an appropriate balance between the independence of the regulator and its accountability, including the expression of expectations through government statements and legislation and, more broadly, a set of formal and less formal but equally important instruments, such as:

- *Publicly available corporate and strategic plans*, sometimes involving input from stakeholders, and policy documents outlining processes (e.g. enforcement policies, pricing principles, decision making procedures).

- *Rigorous* ex ante *assessment and* ex post *assessment of decisions*.

- *Publicly available market assessments* based on information gathered through the agency's operational activities that may be used to provide insights into the performance of the sector and therefore into the regulator's impact.

Clarity of the role of the regulator and how the regulator interacts with other institutions within government are equally important. Lack of clarity on the respective roles creates "grey areas" where the decisions on policy priorities and objectives (the responsibility of elected governments) are mixed with regulatory decisions that should contribute to achieving these objectives. Effective co-ordination translates roles into practice, helps ensure the effectiveness of the regulatory regime, and can reduce unnecessary burdens on the regulated entities while improving compliance.

It is difficult to build effective accountability frameworks and co-ordination mechanisms without the strong commitment of senior management. Management commitment is essential to ensure cultural acceptance of accountability and transparency throughout the organisation and make co-ordination arrangements work in practice. The effectiveness of these governance arrangements would be weakened if formal requirements are met but lack of managerial and board commitment leads to poor implementation.

The practices presented in this report can help guide how accountability, transparency and co-ordination are translated into practice:

- *A proactive regulator detailing actions to meet expectations*: clarity and transparency on what is expected from regulators are crucial. The regulator need to be proactive in identifying the practical steps that will be taken to meet these expectations. Clarity can be achieved through publicly available corporate and strategic plans that detail in a clear and intelligible way what operational modalities and resources the regulators will use to meet these expectations (whether expressed in government statements or legislation).

- *Clear, comprehensive and useful annual reports*: annual reports provide an overview of progress in meeting the regulators' objectives and expectations. They detail what has been done and achieved over the reporting period and therefore complete the information loop that starts with the corporate and strategic plans.

- *Supreme audit institutions and a whole-of-government perspective*: beyond the certification of the regulator's accounts, supreme audit institutions can play a useful role in assessing the performance of the regulated sector, building on the government-wide mandate and expertise.

- *Transparent advice to government and parliament*: regulators are competent and expert actors in the policy making process, building on their in-depth technical knowledge of the sector they regulate. These contributions of the regulator to the policy-making process should be transparent and respect the respective roles of government and regulators.

- *Targeted and useful performance information*: producing and using performance information is challenging. This information needs to be targeted to the purpose it serves. Information and performance indicators prepared to report on budget expenditures will inevitably tend to focus more on direct outputs and inputs than on wider market outcomes. Ideally, oversight bodies, including parliaments, should have access to both types in an intelligible and clear way and be made aware of the challenges in measuring and attributing outcomes.

- *Accessible and assessable information*: simply uploading information onto a website will hardly enhance accountability and transparency. Information needs to be intelligible, clear and user-friendly for citizens, to whom all public institutions are ultimately accountable. Consumer guides and easy-to-access website information should be complemented with activities aimed at actively reaching out and engaging with users.

- *Clarity of roles to avoid institutional and co-ordination gaps*: co-ordination needs to build on some boundaries that define the perimeters of action so that each player – regulators, ministries and other government agencies – is clear on its role or, when grey areas exist, can clarify these grey areas. These roles and perimeters should be set in legally binding instruments to which players (and other stakeholders) can easily refer.

- *The "ground rules" for co-ordination*: formal agreements and co-operation arrangements can set the "ground rules" around which players interact among themselves. They can further clarify respective roles (when they are not sufficiently clear in legislation) and establish regular and structured co-ordination mechanisms. They need to be operationalised through "live" instruments, such as co-ordination bodies, ad hoc meetings, and tools for regular sharing of information.

- *Fit-for-purpose co-ordination instruments*: co-ordination is a large part of the work of the regulator, starting with the inputs provided for relevant regulation and legislation and continuing through the daily oversight of the sector. There is no single instrument that can be used in all these different stages; each instrument needs to be adapted to the objectives that co-ordination seeks to achieve.

# Chapter 1

## The governance of regulators: overview and trends

*This chapter presents an overview of the governance of regulators, drawing on the OECD Best Practice Principles on the Governance of Regulators. It identifies some general trends related to accountability, transparency and co-ordination.*

## Overview

The importance of the governance of regulators is recognised in the *Recommendation on Regulatory Policy and Governance* (Figure 1.1), that invites countries to "develop a consistent policy covering the role and functions of regulatory agencies in order to provide greater confidence that regulatory decisions are made on an objective, impartial, and consistent basis, without conflict of interest, bias or improper influence" (OECD, 2012).

The *OECD Best Practice Principles on the Governance of Regulators* (hereafter the Principles) develop this recommendation by laying out the different building blocks that make up the governance architecture of regulators (Figure 1.1), looking at both:

- *External governance* (looking out from the regulator), focussing on the roles, relationships and distribution of powers and responsibilities between the legislature, the minister, the ministry, the judiciary, the regulator's governing body and regulated entities; and

- *Internal governance* (looking into the regulator), focussing on the regulator's organisational structures, standards of behaviour and role and responsibilities, compliance and accountability measures, oversight of business processes, financial reporting and performance management (OECD, 2014).

The Principles identify a set of high-level objectives at which governments and regulators should aim. They also provide some guidance on how these objectives can be achieved. The guidance attached to each Principle provides some key questions government and regulators should address when applying the Principles to take into consideration the specific industry to be regulated, the political system and the institutional context of each country. This guidance can benefit from insights on the actual practices of regulators. The rest of this section presents some of these insights on a global scale, looking at some general trends underlying the practices of accountability, transparency and co-ordination. Chapter 2 goes on to present some specific practices of regulators.

Figure 1.1. **OECD Best Practice Principles on the Governance of Regulators**

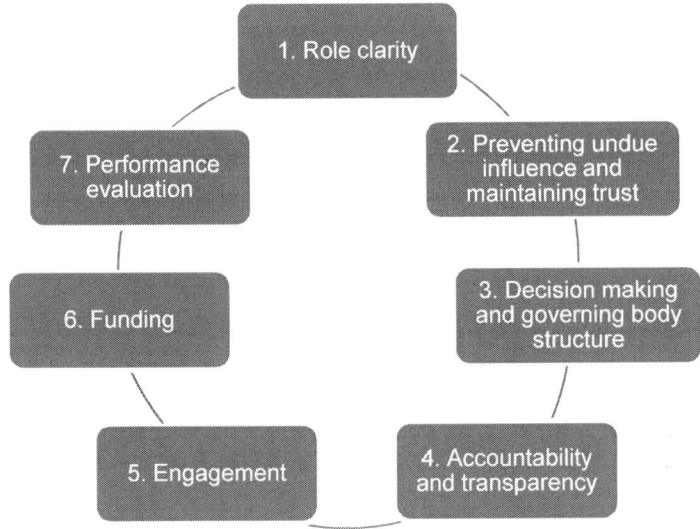

*Source*: Adapted from OECD (2014), *The Governance of Regulators*, OECD Best Practice Principles for Regulatory Policy, OECD Publishing. http://dx.doi.org/10.1787/9789264209015-en.

## Global trends

Work conducted by the OECD across countries and sectors suggests that how accountability is translated into practice can be closely related to the independence of the regulator and its functions and powers. Moreover, regardless of legal requirements, regulators can develop practices and approaches that best fit their needs and contextual challenges.

### *Accountability and scope of action: the Product Market Regulation dataset*

In 2013, the Product Market Regulation (PMR) database was enriched with indicators on the governance of regulators.[1] Regulators responsible for energy (gas and electricity), telecommunications and transport (rail, airports and ports) have provided information on independence, accountability and scope of action through a survey that tracks the implementation of some of the governance arrangements identified in the Principles, with a focus on *de jure*/formal arrangements (OECD, 2016). Answers have been used to produce scores for each component that varies from 0 (the most effective governance structure) to 6 (the least effective governance structure). The scores and the underlying data are available on the OECD website.[2]

A simple correlation of the scores provides some interesting insights on the relationship between some of the Principles. Accountability and independence are positively correlated, suggesting that accountability structures tend to depend to some degree on the formal relationship with the executive.[3] More independent regulators will tend to have stronger accountability structures. At the same time, as the scores for some of the sectors of the regulators included in the case studies regulators suggest, the executive tends to maintain a relatively larger control over the regulators that have a comparatively wider scope of functions and powers (Table 1.1).

Table 1.1. **Correlating independence, accountability and scope of action**

|  | Independence | Accountability | Scope of action |
|---|---|---|---|
| **All sectors:** | | | |
| • Independence | 1 | 0.1 | 0.0 |
| • Accountability |  | 1 | 0.3 |
| **Electricity:** | | | |
| • Independence | 1 | 0.2 | -0.1 |
| • Accountability |  | 1 | 0.3 |
| **Rail:** | | | |
| • Independence | 1 | 0.1 | -0.1 |
| • Accountability |  | 1 | 0.3 |

*Source*: OECD PMR Database, www.oecd.org/economy/growth/indicatorsofproductmarketregulationhomepage.htm (accessed 24 July 2015).

The PMR survey also shows that regulators perform at least some of their activities with other regulators and/or ministries. This is most common for the review of approval of contract terms between regulated entities, enforce compliance and solve disputes between regulated entities/market actors (Figure 1.2).

Figure 1.2. **Regulators' scope of action**

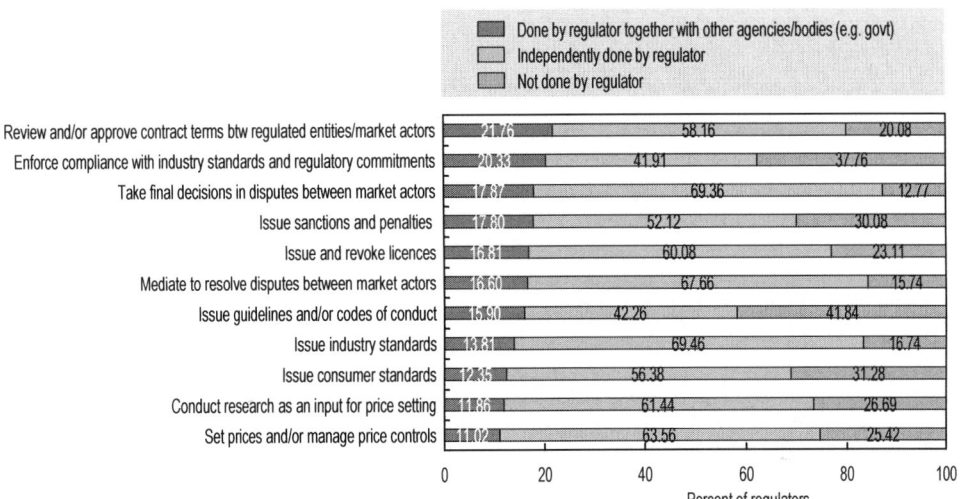

*Source*: OECD PMR Database,
www.oecd.org/economy/growth/indicatorsofproductmarketregulationhomepage.htm (accessed 24 July 2015).

## *Co-ordination mechanisms: the OECD Survey on the Governance of Regulators*

To complement the information collected for the PMR database and provide at the same time greater insights on some of the practices developed to implement the Principles, the OECD carried out a survey of water regulators between September 2013 and September 2014 to investigate the following areas: i) institutional setting; ii) mandates, roles and core regulatory functions; iii) internal organisation; iv) accountability mechanisms; and v) use of tools and mechanisms to ensure regulatory quality. The resulting database covers 34 regulators from 24 countries: 16 in Europe, 11 in the Americas, 2 in Asia (Indonesia and Malaysia), 4 in Oceania (Australia) and 1 in Africa (Mozambique) (OECD, 2015).

Findings from the survey show that information sharing and formal agreements with other bodies are the most common co-operation mechanism mandated by legislation, followed by formal agreements with other bodies sharing some responsibilities for the relevant sector or industry (Figure 1.3).

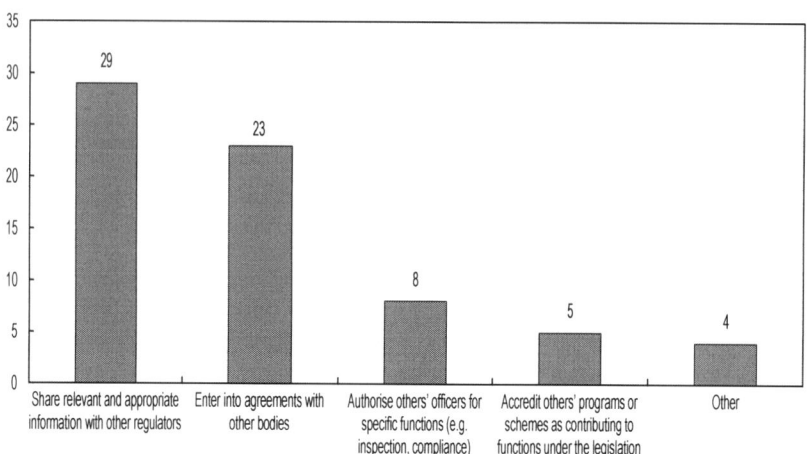

Figure 1.3. **Water regulators: legislative requirements for co-ordination**

*Source*: OECD (2015), *The Governance of Water Regulators*, OECD Studies on Water, OECD Publishing, Paris, http://dx.doi.org/10.1787/9789264231092-en.

Nevertheless, legislative requirements can be translated into practice in different ways. Water regulators appear to have a preference for ad hoc meetings on specific issues (rather than regular meetings or the use of an electronic platform to facilitate real-time information exchange). Moreover, while agreements are required for 23 regulators, only 14 have entered into these agreements (Figure 1.4).

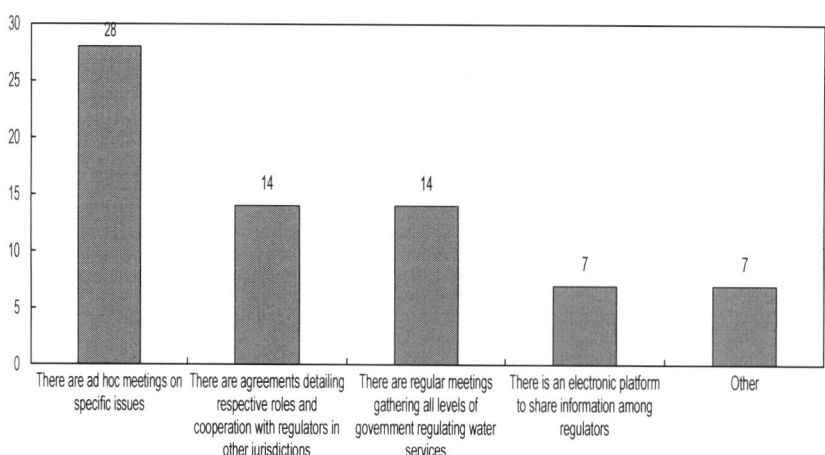

Figure 1.4. **Water regulators: co-ordination practices**

*Source*: OECD (2015), *The Governance of Water Regulators*, OECD Studies on Water, OECD Publishing, Paris, http://dx.doi.org/10.1787/9789264231092-en.

# Notes

1. The PMR dataset estimates economy-wide and sector-related regulatory provisions across countries.

2. OECD (n.d.), "PMR Indicators of Product Market Regulation", www.oecd.org/economy/growth/indicatorsofproductmarketregulationhomepage.htm (accessed 24 July 2015).

3. The direction of the correlation can be considered more important that the magnitude. A correlation coefficient between 0 and 0.5 is usually classified as a "weak correlation", which, however, should not surprise given the many economic and contextual factors that can affect the governance of regulators.

## Bibliography

OECD (2016), "The Global Pictures of Economic Regulators: Independence, Accountability and Scope of Action", *OECD Economics Department Working Papers*, OECD Publishing, Paris, forthcoming.

OECD (2015), *The Governance of Water Regulators*, OECD Studies on Water, OECD Publishing, Paris, http://dx.doi.org/10.1787/9789264231092-en

OECD (2014), *The Governance of Regulators*, OECD Best Practice Principles for Regulatory Policy, OECD Publishing. http://dx.doi.org/10.1787/9789264209015-en.

OECD (2012), *Recommendation of the Council on Regulatory Policy and Governance*, OECD Publishing, Paris, http://dx.doi.org/10.1787/9789264209022-en.

*Chapter 2*

**Regulators' practices**

*This chapter offers an overview of the formal and practical arrangements related to accountability, transparency and co-ordination put in place by the Australian Competition & Consumer Commission (ACCC), the Australian Energy Regulator (AER), Portugal's Water and Waste Services Regulation Authority (ERSAR) and the UK Office of Rail and Road (ORR). It then identifies some guiding lessons that can help guide the implementation of accountability, transparency and co-ordination.*

To look in greater details at how the practices identified across countries are implemented at the level of individual regulators, this section focuses on four regulators – Australia's ACCC and AER, Portugal's ERSAR and the UK's ORR (Box 2.1) – and looks at how they have implemented some of the elements of accountability, transparency and co-ordination identified in the *OECD Best Practice Principles on the Governance of Regulators*. The ACCC, the AER and the ORR provide insights on accountability and transparency practices and ERSAR mostly on co-ordination practices (although some of the accountability and transparency practices described for the ACCC, the AER and the ORR are in place also for ERSAR). Detailed case studies on which this section draws are presented in Chapters 3, 4, and 5.

---

Box 2.1. **The ACCC, AER, ESAR and ORR:
What they are and what they do**

**ACCC**

The Australian Competition & Consumer Commission (ACCC) has a broad range of regulatory, competition and consumer protection functions. Under its broad umbrella reside the Australian national competition enforcement agency, the national consumer protection agency, national product safety standards and enforcement agency, and a suite of regulatory functions, including telecommunications, the Murray-Darling Basin irrigation region, certain rail infrastructure and various sectors which are monitored or in which the ACCC provides advice to government on some charges (e.g. Air Services Australia charges on airport services; Australia Post on letter prices).

**AER**

The Australian Energy Regulator (AER) is the national energy regulator. The AER's enabling legislation is within the Competition and Consumer Act (CCA). However, the AER regulates energy markets and networks under the national energy market (NEM) legislation and rules. Its functions include setting the revenue which can be recovered by network owners from their customers charged for using energy networks (electricity poles and wires and gas pipelines) to transport energy to customers; regulating retail energy markets and enforcing compliance with retail legislation in the Australian Capital Territory, Queensland, South Australia, Tasmania (electricity only) and New South Wales; and monitoring wholesale energy markets and enforcing compliance with the gas and electricity legislation.

> Box 2.1. The ACCC, AER, ESAR and ORR:
> What they are and what they do (*cont.*)
>
> **ERSAR**
>
> Portugal's Water and Waste Services Regulation Authority (ERSAR) is tasked with the economic regulation of drinking water supply services, wastewater management services and municipal waste management services. It is also the national authority for drinking water quality. It is an independent authority with binding powers regarding the regulation of operators and an advisory role to the government on national strategies and legislation. Its independence is explicitly stated in law. It has the power to issue binding regulations without having to obtain approval from other bodies, including government. ERSAR regulations cover topics such as tariffs and economic regulation, quality of service regulation, drinking water quality, user interface and regulatory compliance.
>
> **ORR**
>
> The ORR is the UK economic, safety and health regulator of the rail industry. It is an independent body with a range of functions stated in various acts, along with the associated duties that govern the public interest aspects of those functions. In addition to the more traditional role as an economic regulator of monopoly infrastructure, the ORR is also the national safety regulator for the industry and is the consumer and competition authority, working with the Competition and Markets Authority (CMA) in its application of the 1998 Competition Act where it relates to railways. From 1 April 2015 the ORR took on new responsibilities for overseeing the performance of Highways England, the government-owned company that runs the highways network in England (Wales, Scotland and Northern Ireland have separate arrangements), changing its name from Office of Rail Regulation to Office of Rail and Road. Legislation also mandates ORR to provide advice and assistance to the Secretary of State for Transport, Scottish Ministers and the National Assembly of Wales.
>
> *Source*: Chapters 3, 4 and 5 of the current report.

## Comparability across regulators

These four regulators operate in a governance environment for network regulators that is rather similar in terms of formal independence and accountability, but with some differences in terms of the scope of action of the regulators (especially for the United Kingdom, where regulators tend to have relatively more power and functions). Figure 2.1 shows the average score for the formal governance arrangements for all sectors covered in the PMR dataset for each case study country plus Mexico. In the case of

Australia, the PMR score reflects the context specific expression of independence, accountability and scope of action within Australia which is demonstrated by the established practices and processes in place rather than the formal and codified requirements. While water is not included in the PMR survey, there is a strong positive correlation across governance arrangements for sector regulators within one country (OECD, 2016). Moreover, since 2013, all regulators in Portugal operates under the same institutional and legislative framework.[1] It is therefore assumed that the data would also broadly reflect ERSAR's governance.

Figure 2.1. **The governance of regulators in Australia, Mexico, Portugal and the United Kingdom**

PMR score from 0 (most effective governance structure) to 6 (least effective governance structure)

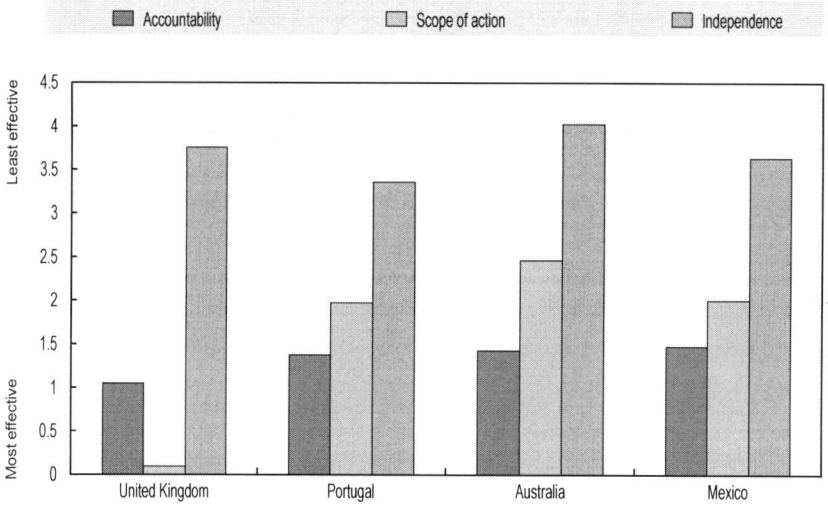

*Note*: The PMR score builds on information provided by regulators responsible for energy (gas and electricity), telecommunications and transport (rail, airports and ports) who responded to a survey on formal arrangements related to independence, accountability and scope of action. Answers have been used to produce scores for each component that varies from 0 (the most effective governance structure) to 6 (the least effective governance structure).

*Source*: OECD PMR Database, www.oecd.org/economy/growth/indicatorsofproductmarketregulationhomepage.htm (accessed 24 July 2015).

These similarities and differences suggest:

- A relatively strong degree of comparability in terms of formal arrangements at least on two correlated elements like independence and accountability;
- A useful practice dataset for identifying different practices in similar formal governance contexts.

## Accountability and transparency

### Accountability and transparency to the minister and legislature

#### Setting expectations for the regulator

Clarity and transparency on government expectations over the work of the regulator can be achieved through different modalities – a formal government statement for the ACCC and the AER and legislation for the ORR. The choice of modality may to some extent depend on the institution to which the regulator is formally accountable. Whatever the modality chosen, the regulator takes a proactive role in making clear what its role and duties are and in identifying the practical steps that will be taken to meet these expectations through publicly-available plans that detail operational modalities and resources deployed.

The ACCC and AER are formally accountable to parliament through the responsible ministers. The government sets expectations in formal Statements of Expectations (SoE) that are publicly available on the Australian Treasury website.[2] These SoE are relatively short – approximately three pages each for the ACCC and the AER – and lay out government expectations on process (e.g. use of better regulation tools and attention for administrative burden reduction) rather than on specific regulatory issues. The regulators respond through a Statement of Intent (SoI) – also available on the Australian Treasury website (Box 2.2).[3] The ACCC also lays out its role, functions, accountability structure and procedures in a relatively short and yet comprehensive brochure available on its website (ACCC, n.d.).

The ORR is solely accountable to Parliament. While members of the ORR Board are appointed by the executive, they are not accountable to the appointing minister, who can only provide "advice" through a published letter (which rarely happens). In the absence of any SE from the executive, the ORR's functions, duties and powers are stated in its current legislation and are accessible via the ORR's website, which provides a clear statement of the ORR's duties.[4]

> **Box 2.2. The Australian government's Statement of Expectations and the regulators' Statement of Intent**
>
> The Australian government's Statement of Expectations (SoE) outlines its expectations about the role and responsibilities of the ACCC, its relationship with the government, issues of transparency and accountability and operational matters. It forms part of the government's commitment to good corporate governance of agencies and reducing the regulatory burden on business and the community. The SoE states that it is imperative that the ACCC act independently and objectively in performing its functions and exercising its powers as set out in the CCA and that the government expects that the ACCC will take into account the government's broad policy framework, in performing its role and meeting its responsibilities. The ACCC in turn provides a Statement of Intent (SoI) outlining how it proposes to meet these expectations.
>
> The AER has a similar SoE with the Council of Australian Governments Energy Council (COAG EC) in which COAG EC outlines its expectations that the AER will perform its legislative functions and implement a work program that supports the objectives set out in the national energy legislation. The AER's SoI sets out the AER's work program in regulating energy networks and markets, and the benchmarks that will measure the AER's performance. The Statement also sets out how it aims to achieve principles of accountability and transparency, efficient regulation and effective engagement with stakeholders and other energy markets.
>
> *Source*: Chapter 3 of the current report.

Actions to meet expectations are detailed in annual plans that are published on the regulators' websites. The ACCC and AER prepare a Corporate Plan that identifies the specific strategies, measures and resources that the regulator will deploy to meet expectations and achieve goals and also includes specific performance indicators to track progress. The ORR publishes an Annual Business Plan as a response to the expectations set in the legislation. The Annual Business Plan provides the strategic objectives and a number of measures, both quantitative and qualitative in order to reach these objectives. It identifies medium and long term outcomes under each strategic objective, and matches it with the annual activities that will help achieve these outcomes (Box 2.3). ERSAR also prepares an activity plan that is submitted for opinion to an Advisory Council composed of key stakeholders, before its submission to the executive and parliament.

> **Box 2.3. Planning ahead to meet expectations at the ACCC, AER and the ORR**
>
> The ACCC and AER Corporate Plan for 2015-16 identifies four strategic objectives. Better regulation is addressed through specific performance indicators developed by the Australian government for all major regulators (the Regulator Performance Framework). For each strategic objective, the Corporate Plan lays out:
>
> - Financial resources and staffing
> - Priorities/programmes
> - Performance indicators for each of the priorities/programmes
>
> The ORR Business Plan for 2015-16 is structured around 6 strategic objectives. Organisational performance and better regulation is one of the strategic objectives ("Be a high-performing regulator"). For each of the 6 strategic objectives, the Business Plan outlines:
>
> - Long-term outcome
> - Medium-term outcomes and outputs
> - Activities
>
> *Source*: ACCC and AER (2015), "Corporate Plan and Priorities 2015-16", https://www.accc.gov.au/publications/corporate-plan-priorities/corporate-plan-priorities-2015-16 (accessed 24 July 2015); ORR (2015), "Business Plan 2015-16", March 2015, http://orr.gov.uk/__data/assets/pdf_file/0018/17622/business-plan-2015-16.pdf (accessed 24 July 2015).

## *Regular reporting to ministries or legislative bodies*

Despite differences in the institution(s) to which the regulator is accountable, for the ACCC, the AER, the ORR and ERSAR, the annual report on the activities completed is the key tool for reporting to oversight institutions. Annual reports provide a high degree of visibility in terms of financial accountability and in ensuring that regulators provide information on their operations. In particular, the ACCC, the AER and the ORR annual reports provide an overview of progress in meeting the regulators' objectives, thus providing some of the essential information that oversight institutions would need to hold regulators accountable (Box 2.4).

> **Box 2.4. Reports to parliament and ministers**
>
> The ORR annual report is addressed to Parliament and identifies some of the key actions that the regulator has undertaken to meet the strategic objectives identified in the business plan.
>
> The ERSAR annual report is addressed to both the executive and parliament. An Advisory Council composed of key government and non-government stakeholders provides an opinion on the report before the submission to the oversight bodies.
>
> The ACCC and the AER annual reports are addressed to the executive. The reports provide an easy-to-read overview of performance towards meeting the key goals set by the ACCC and AER in the corporate plan. The reports also provide information on cases litigated and their outcomes, infringement notices paid, use of agency coercive powers, mergers. Reporting on performance uses a framework that details:
>
> - Performance drivers
> - Objectives
> - Programmes in place to achieve these objectives
>     - Programme objectives
>     - Goals
>
> *Source*: ORR (2015), "Annual Report and Accounts 2014-15", http://orr.gov.uk/__data/assets/pdf_file/0019/18154/annual-report-2014-15-web.pdf (accessed 24 July 2015); ACCC and AER (2014), "Annual Report 2013-14", https://www.accc.gov.au/publications/accc-aer-annual-report/accc-aer-annual-report-2013-14 (accessed 24 July 2015).

Supreme audit institutions (SAIs) also play an important role in providing a third-party check on the financial performance of the regulator. At a minimum, SAIs can be the financial auditors of the regulator. The UK National Audit Office (NAO) certifies the financial statements of the ORR. The Australian National Audit Office (ANAO) is the mandated auditor for the ACCC and AER. Its purpose is to provide the Parliament with an independent assessment of selected areas of public administration, and assurance about public sector financial reporting, administration, and accountability. This is primarily done by conducting performance audits, financial statement audits, and assurance reviews, ensuring the financial accounts. In Portugal, the *Tribunal de Contas* is the auditor for ERSAR.

The role of SAIs can go beyond the certification of the regulators' accounts and, depending on the SAI's mission and role across the public sector, SAIs can assess the performance of the regulator in the relation to other public bodies that are involved in the sector/industry overseen by the regulator. For example, in 2011, the NAO recognised that the ORR had significantly developed the methods it uses to judge efficiency but the effectiveness of these methods depended on the information provided by the publicly-owned rail network monopoly (NAO, 2011).

Regulators' financial resources are usually allocated through the national budget, whose preparation and execution provide another tool that parliaments have to hold regulators accountable. The ACCC, AER and the ORR report on appropriations and spending in the respective annual reports. In Australia, the Portfolio Budget Statement (PBS) is the government public document which explains government's decisions and provides the basis for the hearings where members of parliament can question expenditures according to the deliverables of the government departments and regulatory agencies, including the ACCC and the AER. The PBS links resources to the strategic direction of the relevant agency and to a set of key programme deliverables.[5] This outcomes and outputs framework was introduced for all government departments and agencies with the 1999-2000 budget (Blöndal et al., 2008). This approach developed further in 2014 with the introduction of the Commonwealth Performance Framework that puts strong emphasis on linking together resourcing, planning, results and reporting activities of all government departments and agencies, including regulators.[6]

Regulators also inform and brief oversight institutions on their activities and, beyond their statutory requirements, they can provide advice on issues related to their activities. Reporting on advice provided can be a useful way to enhance mutual accountability. For example, the ORR provides expertise and inputs to parliamentary committees and publishes on its website written statements provided to parliamentary committees.[7] Information on inputs provided to parliamentary committees is also presented in the ORR annual report (Box 2.5). Similarly, ERSAR is periodically requested to participate in public hearings with members of parliament. The ACCC Chairman meets regularly with the ACCC's responsible Minister and/or the Minister's office to provide updates on ACCC activities and matters of significance to the government. In addition, the AER reports biannually to relevant ministers on work activities, key market outcomes and reform proposals. The AER Chair and CEO also attend the meetings of the COAG EC to discuss energy market and network regulation issues.[8] ERSAR's Board of Directors also meet with the Minister of Environment to assess topics of common interest and analyse sector-related policies.

> **Box 2.5. ORR advice and expertise to parliament**
>
> Over the period 2014-15, ORR contributions to the parliamentary process included senior ORR officials giving oral and written evidence to the Transport Select Committee inquiries, including, 'Investing in the Railway' and 'Rail Network Disruption over Christmas 2014' as well as to the Parliamentary Advisory Council for Transport Safety on safety in the railways. The ORR also provided support to Parliament in reaching its decision to confer new duties on it through the Infrastructure Act 2015. This included submitting evidence to the "Better Road' inquiries and providing various briefings to parliamentarians. ORR also contributed expertise to parliamentary debate through a programme of engagement to promote better understanding and greater transparency of the railways amongst members and Parliament and their staff. This included an open briefing session held jointly with the Royal Statistical Society and the House of Commons Library and participation in All Party Parliamentary Group discussions on occupational health and rail.
>
> *Source*: ORR (2015), "Annual Report and Accounts 2014-15", http://orr.gov.uk/__data/assets/pdf_file/0019/18154/annual-report-2014-15-web.pdf (accessed 24 July 2015).

## *Development of performance indicators to monitor the effectiveness of the regulatory regime*

Performance indicators are essential to help the regulator measure its performance and, through these indicators, help government measure the effectiveness of regulatory regimes for which elected governments are ultimately responsible. This is an area where challenges can be significant, starting with what to measure to attributing causal links and producing data.[9] The ACCC, the AER, ERSAR and the ORR have developed performance indicators, whose scope and use can nevertheless vary depending on the reporting requirements, accountability structures and the overall approach to performance measurement.

Similar to all other regulatory agencies and government departments, the ACCC and AER have developed performance indicators under each priority/programme. These indicators are included in the appropriation request – the PBS – submitted by the Treasury to parliament. The Corporate Plan and the AER's SoI set specific targets for each of these indicators, which are then monitored through the Annual Reports. The AER has specific performance indicators (Box 2.6) and prepares a 'traffic light report', highlighting where the AER does not meet performance targets and outlining measures to improve performance.

## Box 2.6. AER selected performance indicators

**Provide effective network regulation**

- Number of revenue reset determinations for electricity networks and gas pipelines and distribution networks completed
- Percentage of revenue reset determinations for electricity networks and gas pipelines and distribution networks completed within statutory timeframes
- Number of annual benchmarking and performance reports for electricity networks
- Number of annual tariff approval applications assessed

**Build consumer confidence in retail energy markets**

- Number of retailers' hardship policies and proposed amendments assessed (externally driven)
- Percentage of retailers' hardship policies and proposed amendments assessed within 12 weeks of receiving all relevant information
- Number of retail authorisations/exemptions assessed (externally driven)
- Percentage of retail authorisations/exemptions applications assessed within 12 weeks of receiving all relevant information
- Support the timely transfer of affected customers in the event of a retailer failure (externally driven)
- Number of formal energy retail enforcement interventions (court proceeding commenced, s. 288 (NERL) undertakings accepted, infringement notices issued) (externally driven)
- Percentage of new/replacement offers published on Energy Made Easy website within 48 hours of receipt from retailers

**Support efficient wholesale energy markets**

- Number of quarterly compliance reports on wholesale markets and networks
- Percentage of quarterly compliance reports published within six weeks of the end of the quarter
- Audit the compliance systems of selected energy businesses, and report on outcomes

> **Box 2.6. AER selected performance indicators** (*cont.*)
>
> - Number of weekly electricity and gas monitoring reports
>
> - Percentage of weekly reports published within 12 business days of the end of the relevant week
>
> - Number of reports on extreme price events in wholesale electricity and gas markets (externally driven)
>
> - Percentage of reports on extreme price events in wholesale electricity and gas markets published within statutory timeframes
>
> - Number of targeted reviews of compliance with the national energy rules (as measured by number of reports)
>
> - Publish the State of the energy market report
>
> *Source*: ACCC and AER (2015), "Corporate Plan and Priorities 2015-16", https://www.accc.gov.au/publications/corporate-plan-priorities/corporate-plan-priorities-2015-16 (accessed 24 July 2015).

Starting in July 2015, a Regulator Performance Framework (RPF) assesses Commonwealth entities that have a statutory responsibility to administer, monitor, or enforce regulation against six common performance indicators focusing on good regulatory performance/better regulation to complement the regulator-specific performance indicators (Box 2.7). The six common performance indicators are the following:

- regulators do not unnecessarily impede the efficient operation of regulated entities;

- communication with regulated entities is clear, targeted and effective;

- actions taken by regulators are proportionate to the risk being managed;

- compliance and monitoring approaches are streamlined and co-ordinated;

- regulators are open and transparent in their dealings with regulated entities; and

- regulators actively contribute to the continuous improvement of regulatory frameworks.

> **Box 2.7. Australia's Regulator Performance Framework**
>
> Two current governance reform programmes being implemented by the Australian Commonwealth Government (the Commonwealth) are of particular relevance to the issues of accountability and transparency. The Commonwealth Performance Framework is a broad based program aimed at all government departments and agencies while the Regulator Performance Framework (RPF) is aimed at regulators only. The programs are both based in large part on calls from government and other stakeholders for increased accountability and transparency in the operations of government entities.
>
> The ACCC is subject to both performance frameworks. In recognition of specific accountability framework already operating under the COAG Energy Council – which is consistent with the RPF – the AER is subject only to the CPF.
>
> The RPF aims to encourage regulators to minimise their impact on those they regulate while still delivering the vital role they have been asked to perform. Australian government regulators will self-assess their performance against the Framework annually. A number of regulators will be subject to an external review of their performance as part of a three year programme, and a small number of regulators may be subject to an annual external review. External reviews will be conducted by review panels of government and industry representatives to provide further accountability, and provide additional transparency for stakeholders and the community in general. The Framework is based on a report by the Productivity Commission and was developed in consultation with regulators and stakeholders. The Framework will apply from 1 July 2015.
>
> *Source*: Chapter 3 of the current report.

The ORR is subject to less stringent requirements in terms of performance indicators as outcomes are not subject to any agreement between the regulators and ministers or parliament. The ORR recognises the difficulties in tracking performance, reflecting to a large extent the fact that a significant aspect of the regulator's work is to ensure the prevention of harm, which is difficult to measure. The ORR does nevertheless track data that help follow market and industry developments and guide regulatory decisions (beside *ex ante* and *ex post* assessment of major regulatory decisions). For example, it has developed a Public Performance Measure (PPM) that forms part of Network Rail's regulatory outputs, which measures the punctuality of passenger trains, and is presented along with data on safety and investment in a clear format in ORR's Annual Report (Figure 2.2).

### Figure 2.2. Tracking industry performance at ORR

Driving efficiency & supporting investment
Savings of over
£4 billion
of taxpayers' and customers' money identified since 2004 in ORR's Periodic Reviews of Network Rail.
A further 19% reduction
assumed over the current control period to 2019
Network Rail investment in enhancements
x4
OMR Efficiency
£1.7bn
PR13
£2.4bn
PR08
£4.1bn
assumption
+19%
2004
2014
2019
The Regulatory Asset Base (RAB) has supported reinvestment of the proceeds of efficiency to fund a
four-fold increase in investment
in new capacity and services.
Regulating improved performance
ORR has set stretching performance targets in the past 5-10 years and has overseen record levels of punctuality for passenger and freight against a backdrop of sustained growth in customer demand
Between 2001-02 and 2013-14 the Public Performance Measure (PPM) of passenger trains that arrive at final destination on time has increased from 78% to 90%.
90%
2013-14
78%
2001-02
Between 2005-06 and 2013-14, freight punctuality has increased from 65% to 75%
75%
2013-14
65%
2005-06
Requiring continuous improvement in safety
Fatalities per million train km
0.00 0.02 0.04 0.06 0.08 0.10 0.12 0.14 0.16
Bulgaria
Estonia
Belgium
Romania
Portugal
Latvia
Greece
Lithuania
Spain
Poland
Hungary
Czech Republic
Slovakia
Italy
Slovenia
France
Ireland
Austria
Germany
Finland
Sweden
Denmark
Netherlands
United Kingdom
0.003
Luxembourg
EU average
0.026
Normalised workforce fatalities
Normalised passenger fatalities

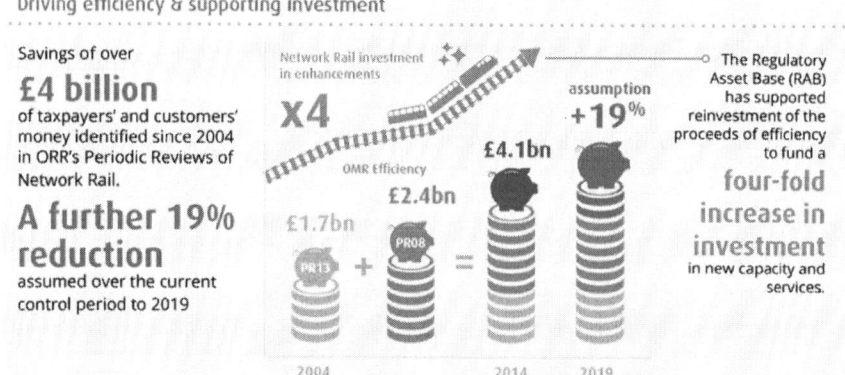

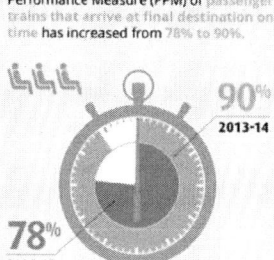

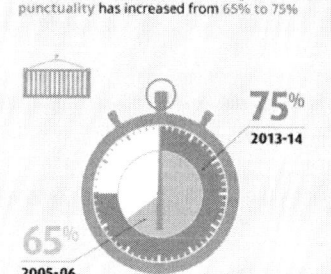

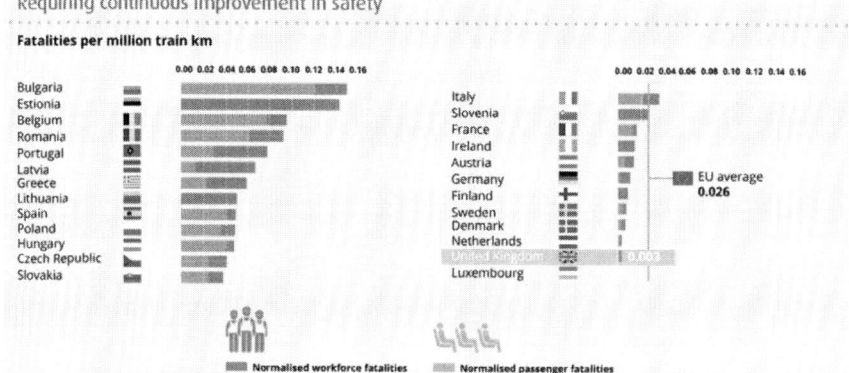

*Source*: ORR (2015), "Annual Report and Accounts 2014-15", http://orr.gov.uk/__data/assets/pdf_file/0019/18154/annual-report-2014-15-web.pdf, p. 38. (accessed 24 July 2015).

Since 2004, ERSAR has been tracking a set of performance indicators on the quality of the service provided by operators. This set of indicators is used to assess the evolution in the sector in terms of the quality that is provided to the users. In 2009, the set of indicators was revised and enhanced to improve the assessment of the quality of the service provided by operators.

### Accountability and transparency to regulated entities and the public

#### Judicial review

The regulator's decisions can be challenged in front of judicial or quasi-judicial bodies independent of the regulator, which can ask the regulator to review its decisions or repeal it altogether. ACCC and AER decisions can be challenged in courts and/or in the Australian Competition Tribunal (ACT).[10] For AER network pricing decisions, business networks can seek a review by the ACT and the AER is a party to the review. The AER must act as a model litigant, using its best endeavours to help the ACT make its decision. The ACT can remit a regulatory decision (or aspects of a decision) to the AER for further consideration. In addition, the courts can review the AER's decisions on administrative grounds. Different aspects of the ORR's regulatory decisions may attract different appeals mechanisms. For example, appeals on regulatory decisions may be undertaken through the High Court (e.g. for access decisions), the Competition Appeals Tribunal[11] (e.g. for competition cases) or the Competition and Market Authority (CMA) (e.g. for the periodic review of network infrastructure). Judicial review also applies to ERSAR's decisions.

#### Public availability of key operational policies and guidance material

Putting information on websites is relatively easy. The effort undertaken by the regulators is to go beyond the sheer provision of information and produce information that is not only accessible but also assessable and well understood by all stakeholders. For example, the ACCC prepares an annual Telecommunications Report that provides an in-depth view on the telecommunications sector and its various services and products. It also provides reports on broader market trends and not just on specific regulatory decisions. While the reports are not directly related to statutory decisions, or obviously part of the individual suite of accountability and transparency measures, they do give observers a clear, year-on-year picture of the market and, to a certain extent, of the impact of the regulatory regime. Similarly, the ORR publishes reports besides regulatory decisions and provides information that can be well understood and interpreted by interested parties. The AER has also established a Stakeholder Engagement

Framework that sets out principles for the provision of clear and understandable communication (Box 2.8).

---

**Box 2.8. The AER's Stakeholder Engagement Framework**

The Stakeholder Engagement Framework aims at building strong and effective communication channels and facilitating understanding by improving the clarity, accessibility, relevance and timeliness of communication with stakeholders. The Framework sets out a set of principles that are published and reported on with a commitment to measure engagement, thus providing a strong discipline on the AER and complementing the range of more formal accountability mechanisms:

- Principle 1: Clear, accurate and timely communication
- Principle 2: Accessible and inclusive
- Principle 3: Transparent
- Principle 4: Measurable

*Source*: Chapter 3 of the current report.

---

*Public access to reasoning behind the regulator's major decisions*

Major decisions made by the ACCC, the AER and the ORR are accessible to the general public via the Internet. Yet, simply making information available is clearly perceived by both regulators as not sufficient to give the public access to why and how decisions can affect consumers. All the regulators take an active role in making information intelligible and usable by the public. For example, the ACCC has developed a suite of *Guides for consumers* that describe in simple, non-technical language how the ACCC sets rules for the supply of telecommunications services.[12] This is part of an effort to inform the public more broadly of the ACCC's role in the telecommunications sector and allow consumers to gain greater clarity on the complex world of telecommunications services and markets and how the ACCC regulates it. Similarly, the ORR strives to provide quality, trusted information on the performance of the sector, costs and funding as fundamental to enabling customers to understand and therefore make judgements on the quality of services, change in fares over time and level of tax payer funds supporting the railway.

## Co-ordination

The Principles identify co-ordination as one of the elements that help regulators fulfil their role effectively. Co-ordination is closely related to the clarity of the purposes and objectives that have been set for the regulator. On co-ordination practices, ERSAR, Portugal's water regulator, provides a particularly interesting case on two grounds:

- the wide scope of ERSAR mandate as it regulates not only drinking water and sanitation but also waste management services, a rather unique feature among water regulators; and
- the wide range of central and local government entities (in addition to a relatively high number of operators) that are involved in the water and waste management sectors.

### *Purposes and objectives of the regulator*

The regulatory framework under which regulators operate tends to change over time to respond to new public policy challenges and priorities. These evolutions can change the functions and roles of the regulator and the bodies and area of competencies on which the regulator needs to co-ordinate. In Portugal, ERSAR was established as part of a broad regulatory reform aimed at building strong, technically efficient, and universal water and waste sectors. The reform was intended to protect the public interest in recognition of the fundamental role water and waste services play in society and to make service providers more accountable. Accordingly, the regulator was given a role in harmonising practices and criteria for service provision, taking over some functions from other government bodies and sharing others with other bodies.

Changes in the regulatory framework tend to happen over extended periods of time, under different governments and sometimes to respond to different needs and priorities. This can create institutional and co-ordination gaps. It is important to clearly state the scope and functions of the regulator in legislation that takes into account this evolution and provides for a clear role and mandate for the regulator. In Portugal, Law No. 10/2014 of 6 March 2014 has adapted ERSAR's statutes to a new, fully independent regulatory framework applied to all utilities regulators, which is particularly important in a relatively complex sector like water with a number of operators and government stakeholders at the central and local level (Box 2.9 and Figure 2.3). In particular, the law has granted ERSAR further independence and additional responsibilities in terms of economic regulation, especially in municipality-managed services. The law incorporates previous legislative evolutions and provides a clear framework for the roles and objectives of the regulator. Initial steps towards the current institutional framework started with the Decree-Law No. 230/97 of 30 August 1997 that established ERSAR's predecessor, the Institute for Regulation of Water & Solid Waste (IRAR). The creation of IRAR responded to reforms introduced in 1993 to address structural, pricing and other strategic issues affecting the Portuguese water supply, urban wastewater and solid waste management. These reforms, among other measures, have created several regional bulk service systems responsible for the extraction and treatment of drinking water and for the treatment and disposal of urban wastewater.[13] The Decree-Law No. 243/2001 of 5 September 2001 extended the remit of IRAR to drinking water quality. In October 2009, Decree-Law No. 277/2009 transformed the IRAR into ERSAR, extending the scope of the regulatory functions.

---

**Box 2.9. The water and waste management sector in Portugal**

State and municipal governments share responsibility for water and waste management services within the Portuguese regulatory framework. The State is responsible for the bulk services (multi-municipal systems) while the retail services are the responsibility of municipalities (municipal systems).[1] Accordingly, ERSAR's remit extends to private owned utilities; state owned utilities, both national and sub-national; all urban water services and rural water services (which include many small scale operators such as local parish and user associations). ERSAR oversees 432 operators in the water and waste management sectors and 326 water supply operators in relation to water quality.

1. Bulk water is usually defined as water supplied by a provider to another provider.

*Source*: Chapter 4 of the current report.

---

A clear and well defined role enshrined in legislation can help improve co-ordination by clearly setting areas of joint competencies where the regulator and other authorities have a clear mandate (and obligation) to co-operate. ERSAR shares joint competencies with three other bodies in clearly defined areas:

- The Portuguese Environmental Agency (APA) for monitoring the environmental sustainability of water and waste management services;

- The Ministry for Environment and Energy (MOATE) for the development of new legislation and strategies;

- The Competition Authority for public procurement procedures for the management of water services; mergers and acquisitions of water operators; expansion of water operators to other non-regulated markets.

Figure 2.3. **Institutional arrangements for water regulation in Portugal**

| National level | Government | Public agencies |
|---|---|---|
| | **Ministry for Environment and Energy (MAOTE)**<br>*Policy definition and strategy; ownership of bulk services* | **Water and waste services regulation authority (ERSAR)** |
| | | **Portuguese Environmental Agency (APA)**<br>*Water planning; water abstraction and discharge licensing* |
| | | **Competition Authority (AdC)**<br>*Enforcement of competition rules* |
| | | **Operator's association** |
| Local level | **Municipalities**<br>*Decision about retail tariffs; ownership of retail services* | |

*Source*: OECD (2015), *The Governance of Water Regulators*, OECD Studies on Water, OECD Publishing, Paris, http://dx.doi.org/10.1787/9789264231092-en.

In addition, ERSAR also needs to deal and co-ordinate with a number of other ministries and government departments involved in planning, finance, health, economic and regional development, as well as municipalities and associations of municipalities.

## *Policy advice*

While formulating policy and regulation is a primary responsibility of elected governments, the advice of the regulator early in the formulation process can provide robust data and evidence on the problems to be addressed and provide a tool for inter-institutional co-ordination. The role of ERSAR in the development of new legislation and strategies is related to technical advice in terms of service provision. This role builds on the information and knowledge that ERSAR has on the water and waste management sectors. This advisory role is usually exercised through the participation of ERSAR in co-ordination meetings organised by the ministry.

## Instruments of co-ordination

Formal agreements and co-operation arrangements can set the "ground rules" for co-ordination and clarify inter-agency boundaries, to be complemented by "live" instruments like co-ordination bodies, regular exchange information and meetings. ERSAR uses formal agreements and co-operation arrangements to co-ordinate with those regulatory authorities with which co-ordination is mandated in legislation. As shown in section 3, formal agreements are common among regulators to share functions with other bodies. The ORR, for example, uses them to transfer certain functions to other agencies in cases where legislation and respective mandates are unclear.[14] Memoranda of Understanding (MoUs) can be also used to lay out roles and functions and facilitate co-ordination (MoUs can have a less binding character than agency agreements).[15] These instruments can have the advantage of further clarifying respective roles (when they are not sufficiently clear in legislation) and establish regular and structured co-ordination mechanisms. Their update may also help take stock of the effectiveness of these mechanisms and adapt them to evolving needs. They can set the ground rules but they need to be operationalised.

The objectives to be achieved by co-ordinating with other regulators and government bodies and the stage at which this co-ordination takes place tend to guide the choice of "live" co-ordination instruments. Table 2.1 classifies ERSAR co-ordination instruments according to the different co-ordination stages and objectives.

ERSAR experience suggests a preference for intense bilateral dialogue in the provision of feedback on policy formulation, the use of permanent and broader advisory bodies for informing and creating buying in across government on the regulator's overall planning and a more technical and continuous exchange of data and information for the daily implementation work. ERSAR and APA have ad hoc technical meetings to forge a common position on sector policies and legislation that is being prepared by the government, with the objective of creating the conditions for clarity and consistency in implementation. When ERSAR is developing its own strategic plan and takes stock of the impact of its activities for the preparation of the Annual Report, the choice is for a permanent consultative body, ERSAR Advisory Council, which brings together representatives of all levels of government (and non-government stakeholders), to facilitate mutual communication at key regular stages of the work of the regulator (and buy-in from other stakeholders). In the daily work of overseeing the water and waste sectors, ERSAR recognises the importance of regular and continuous exchange of information with key bodies with which it shares a joint competence (in particular the APA and the Competition Authority). This is also expected to help avoid imposing unnecessary burden on regulated entities through multiple information requests and inspections. For this purpose, ERSAR set up an information management system to facilitate these exchanges and is working towards greater interconnectivity with the information systems of the other regulatory authorities. It collaborates with other agencies for the collection, validation, processing and dissemination of water services information. It also reports on situations which may indicate the presence of infringements and receive information from other agencies concerning inspection activities carried out on water service utilities.

Table 2.1. **Mapping co-ordination stages, objectives and instruments**

| Stage | Objective | Regulators/government agencies | Instrument |
| --- | --- | --- | --- |
| Formulation of government sector policy and legislation | Joint interpretation of legislation to facilitate clarity and consistency in implementation | Environmental Protection Agency (APA) | Joint technical meetings/common positions |
| Planning of ERSAR activities and stocktaking of implementation | Inform government departments and municipalities and benefit from input and advice | Central and local government, | Permanent consultation mechanism (Advisory Council) The Advisory Council also includes consumers' associations, operators' associations, experts and other non-government stakeholders |
| Implementation/market oversight | Avoid overlapping and unnecessary burden/compliance costs | Environmental Protection Agency (APA) Competition Authority Public Health Authority | Collaboration in the collection, validation, processing and dissemination of water services information Mutual reporting of inspection activities Information Management System (but not yet connected with other agencies' systems) |

*Source*: Chapter 4 of the current report.

## Guiding lessons

The arrangements and practices presented above help identify some lessons that can guide how accountability, transparency and co-ordination are translated into practice:

- *A proactive regulator detailing actions to meet expectations*: clarity and transparency on what is expected from regulators is key as is the role of the regulator in identifying the practical steps that will be taken to meet these expectations. This clarity can be achieved through publicly available corporate and strategic plans that detail in a clear and intelligible fashion what operational modalities and resources the regulators will use to meet these expectations (be they expressed in government statements or legislation).

- *Clear, comprehensive and useful annual reports*: annual reports provide an overview of progress in meeting the regulators' objectives and expectations. They detail what has been done and achieved over the reporting period and therefore close the information loop that opens with the corporate and strategic plans. They are not a simple bureaucratic exercise and need to be clear, structured and backed up by appropriate evidence as they provide some of the essential information that oversight institutions would need in order to hold regulators accountable.

- *Supreme audit institutions and a whole of government perspective*: beyond the certification of the regulator's accounts, supreme audit institutions can play a useful role (for the wider public but also for the regulator) in assessing the performance of the regulated sector, building on the government-wide mandate and expertise.

- *Transparent advice to government and parliament*: regulators are competent and expert actors in the policy making process, building on their in-depth technical knowledge of the sector they regulate. These contributions of the regulator to the policy-making process should be transparent and respect the respective roles of government and regulators.

- *Targeted and useful performance information*: producing and using performance information is challenging. This information needs to be targeted to the purpose it serves. Information and performance indicators prepared to report on budget expenditures will inevitably tend to focus more on direct outputs and inputs than on wider market outcomes. Ideally, oversight bodies, including parliaments, should have access to both in an intelligible and clear way and be made aware of the challenges in measuring and attributing outcomes.

- *Accessible and assessable information*: simply uploading information onto a website will hardly enhance accountability and transparency. Information needs to be intelligible, clear and user-friendly for citizens, to whom all public institutions are ultimately accountable. Consumer guides and easy-to-access website information should be complemented with activities aimed at actively reaching out and engage with users.

- *Clarity of role to avoid institutional and co-ordination gaps*: co-ordination needs to build on some boundaries that define perimeters of action so that each player – regulators, ministries and other government agencies – is clear on its role or, when grey areas exist, can clarify these grey areas. Co-ordination can then effectively help players interact among themselves. These roles and perimeters of action should be set in legally binding instruments to which players (and other stakeholders) can easily refer to.

- *The "ground rules" for co-ordination*: in the co-ordination architecture, formal agreements and co-operation arrangements are a level down from legislation and can set the "ground rules" around which players interact among themselves. They can further clarify respective roles (when they are not sufficiently clear in legislation) and establish regular and structured co-ordination mechanisms. Their update may also help take stock of the effectiveness of co-ordination mechanisms and adapt them to evolving needs. They need to be operationalised though "live" instruments like co-ordination bodies, ad hoc meetings, tools for regular sharing of information.

- *Fit-for-purpose co-ordination instruments*: co-ordination accompanies a large part of the work of the regulator, starting with the inputs provided for relevant regulation and legislation and continuing through the daily oversight of the sector. There is no single instrument that can fit all these different stages; each instrument needs to be adapted to the objectives that co-ordination seeks to achieve. For example, bilateral dialogue and ad hoc meetings can be used to forge common positions across regulators for the provision of feedback on policy formulation. Permanent advisory bodies can help bring together a wider set of government (and non-government stakeholders) to inform and create buying in across government on the regulator's overall planning. Technical and continuous exchange of data and information can be most appropriate for the daily implementation work of the regulators.

# Notes

1. This framework was established by Law No. 67/2013 of 28 August 2013.

2. www.treasury.gov.au/Policy-Topics/PublicPolicyAndGovt/Statements-of-Expectations

3. www.treasury.gov.au/policy-topics/publicpolicyandgovt/~/link.aspx?_id=db7094eb11244c9192e44870f7aed7ac&_z=z.

4. http://orr.gov.uk/about-orr/what-we-do.

5. Australian Government Treasury (2015), "ACCC Portfolio Budget Statement", www.treasury.gov.au/~/media/Treasury/Publications%20and%20Media/Publications/2015/PBS%202015/Downloads/PDF/03_ACCC.ashx (accessed 24 July 2015).

6. Australian Government Department of Finance (n.d.), "Resource management," www.finance.gov.au/resource-management (accessed 24 July 2015).

7. http://orr.gov.uk/about-orr/what-we-do/how-we-work/accountability.

8. The COAG Energy Council is responsible for major energy reform and the national energy legislation. The Council consists of the Commonwealth, State, Territory and New Zealand energy and resources ministers.

9. See OECD, 2015c for an overview of these challenges applied to a regulator, Colombia's Communications Regulator.

10. The Tribunal is a review body that can re-hear or re-consider a matter. The Tribunal may perform all the functions and exercise all the powers of the original decision-maker for the purposes of review. It can affirm, set aside or vary the original decision. See Australian Competition Tribunal (n.d.), "About the Tribunal", www.competitiontribunal.gov.au/about (accessed 24 July 2015).

11. The United Kingdom Competition Appeal Tribunal is a specialist judicial body with cross-disciplinary expertise in law, economics, business and accountancy whose function is to hear and decide cases involving competition or economic regulatory issues. See UK Competition Appeal Tribunal (n.d.), "The Competition Appeal Tribunal", www.catribunal.org.uk/ (accessed 24 July 2015).

12. www.accc.gov.au/regulated-infrastructure/communications/accc-role-in-communications/consumer-fact-sheets-for-telecommunications-services

13. Bulk water (and the related services) is usually defined as water supplied by a provider to another provider.

14. See, for example, the "Agency agreement between Health and Safety Executive (HSE) and ORR on road vehicle incursions" of 27 April 2015, http://orr.gov.uk/__data/assets/pdf_file/0004/17788/agency-agreement-between-hse-and-orr-on-road-vehicle-incursions.pdf (accessed 24 July 2015).

15. ORR (n.d.), "Agency agreements and memoranda of understandings", http://orr.gov.uk/about-orr/who-we-work-with/agency-agreements-and-mous (accessed 24 July 2015).

# Bibliography

ACCC (n.d.), "The Australian Competition & Consumer Commission's accountability framework for investigations", https://www.accc.gov.au/system/files/ACCC%27s%20accountablility%20framework%20for%20investigations.pdf (accessed 24 July 2015).

ACCC and AER (2015), "Corporate Plan and Priorities 2015-16", https://www.accc.gov.au/publications/corporate-plan-priorities/corporate-plan-priorities-2015-16 (accessed 24 July 2015).

Blöndal, J.R. et al. (2008), "Budgeting in Australia", *OECD Journal on Budgeting*, Vol. 8/2, OECD Publishing, Paris, http://dx.doi.org/10.1787/budget-v8-art9-en.

NAO (2011), "Regulating Network Rail's Efficiency", www.nao.org.uk/report/regulating-network-rails-efficiency/ (accessed 24 July 2015).

OECD (2016), "The Global Pictures of Economic Regulators: Independence, Accountability and Scope of Action", *OECD Economics Department Working Papers*, OECD Publishing, Paris, forthcoming.

OECD (2015), *The Governance of Water Regulators*, OECD Studies on Water, OECD Publishing, Paris, http://dx.doi.org/10.1787/9789264231092-en.

ORR (2015), "Annual Report and Accounts 2014-15", http://orr.gov.uk/__data/assets/pdf_file/0019/18154/annual-report-2014-15-web.pdf (accessed 24 July 2015).

## Chapter 3

## Australian Energy Regulator and Australian Competition & Consumer Commission's Telecommunications Regulation

*This chapter presents the arrangements and practices related to accountability and transparence put in place by the Australian Energy Regulator. It then presents some of these arrangements and practices put in place by the Australian Competition & Consumer Commission in relation to telecommunications regulation.*

## Section A: ACCC and AER organisational frameworks

### *Objectives and functions*

This Section outlines features of the regulatory framework and associated accountability and transparency measures that are common to both regulators under the Competition and Consumer Act 2010 (CCA) legislative framework.

The Australian Competition & Consumer Commission (ACCC) covers a broad range of regulatory, competition and consumer protection roles. Under its broad umbrella reside the Australian national competition enforcement agency, the national consumer protection agency, national product safety standards and enforcement agency, and a suite of regulatory functions relating to infrastructure in sectors such as telecommunications, wheat ports, rail and water and various sectors which are monitored or in which the ACCC provides advice to government on some charges (e.g. Air Services Australia charges on airport services; Australia Post on letter prices).

The Australian Energy Regulator (AER) is the national energy regulator. While the AER's enabling legislation is within the CCA, it regulates energy markets and networks under the national energy market (NEM) legislation and rules. Its functions include setting the revenue which can be recovered by network owners from their customers for using energy networks (electricity poles and wires and gas pipelines) to transport energy to customers; regulating retail energy markets and enforcing compliance with retail legislation in the ACT, Queensland, South Australia, Tasmania (electricity only) and New South Wales; and monitoring wholesale energy markets and enforcing compliance with the gas and electricity legislation.

The ACCC was established following the August 1993 *Report by the Independent Committee of Inquiry, National Competition Policy* (otherwise known as the Hilmer Review). In addition to a wide ranging set of recommendations aimed at improving Australia's competitiveness, the report also recommended an institutional model with the ACCC having economy-wide responsibility for economic regulation in addition to competition and consumer protection (Pearson, 2011).

Competition was seen by the authors of the Hilmer Review as the unifying theme bringing the national competition, consumer protection and regulatory functions together. In addition to encouraging a pro-competition culture in regulatory matters, bringing national economic regulation under the auspices of the ACCC, instead of the establishment of industry specific bodies, had the benefit of reducing potential distortions across industries and pooling limited skills and expertise.

The establishment of the AER came after a period of national reforms to open up the traditionally state-controlled gas and electricity sectors that had operated in the main as integrated monopolies. The transformation of these sectors required close collaboration between the Commonwealth (Federal) and State governments, as they fell for the most part under the jurisdiction of the States and Territories. The sectors developed and matured to such an extent that governments realised the regulatory instruments and tools also needed to change and respond.

While the ACCC had separate Electricity and Gas Branches from its establishment in 1995 the growing task and complexity of the developing markets led to further assessment of the institutional arrangements for these sectors. A major factor was the need to have a decision making board able to provide sustainable oversight of the rapidly growing work load as State and Territory governments prepared to hand over their economic regulatory responsibilities to the Commonwealth regulator. Other measures, such as an Energy Committee that included State regulators, had proved unwieldy and were not going to be appropriate in the changing environment.

In 2005 the AER was established with its own independent decision-making Board. While the Australian government agreed to fund the new body, that funding was provided through the ACCC budget allocation as part of its overall outcome as stated in the Portfolio Budget statement (PBS) in line with the Australian government's financial and budget framework:[1]

- Lawful competition, consumer protection, and regulated national infrastructure markets and services through regulation, including enforcement, education, price monitoring and determining the terms of access to infrastructure services.

Sections B and C of the case study take a closer look at the specific regulatory frameworks, objectives and functions of the Telecommunications Group within the ACCC and the AER, in regards to its energy specific responsibilities. The AER in particular has a set of measures in place that flow directly from the nature of the legislative framework for energy regulation and its role as a Commonwealth (i.e. Federal) regulator applying State based laws. This is discussed further in Part 3 of the case study.

Section 2 of the CCA, to which both the AER and ACCC are subject, states that the object of the Act is "to enhance the welfare of Australians through the promotion of competition, fair trading and provision for consumer protection". While the object clause informs interested parties of the broad object of the Act each particular regulatory regime also operates under specific legal frameworks, which, while similar in many respects, also reflect differences in market structures, maturity, technology and services being delivered.

While the regimes differ there is a common object (Gray, 2013):

- To promote the economically efficient operation of, use of, and investment in infrastructure; and

- In turn, promote competition in dependent markets, and the long term interests of end-users.

In addition the regulatory regimes broadly recognise that:

- A regulated entity should expect to recover its efficient costs;

- The expected return should be commensurate with the risks; and

- A regulated entity should be provided with incentives to promote efficiency.

The following case studies focus on these objectives with a more in-depth consideration of the energy and telecommunications regimes and the particular functions and responsibilities that each regulatory framework entails, including the sector specific objectives. While each framework has its own set of requirements, the ACCC and AER more broadly undertake a substantial body of work in addressing accountability responsibilities and in ensuring transparency of decisions, guidance, and reporting and key performance indicators.

Corporate plans; annual reports; guidance material; reporting on decisions; public forums; publication of draft discussion and decision papers; are all part of the overall formal and informal accountability and transparency framework of the ACCC and AER. As will be noted in the case study, the model does create some specific challenges in regards to accountability and transparency, particularly in respect to the AER.

## *Organisation*

As noted, the ACCC is an independent statutory authority that enforces the Competition and Consumer Act 2010 (CCA) and other legislation. The ACCC has a range of regulatory functions in relation to national infrastructure sectors, in addition to its competition and consumer protection roles. It performs a prices oversight role in some markets where competition is limited in addition to the more direct regulatory role identified in above in telecommunications, post, irrigated water, rail, ports (including monitoring of stevedores), fuel and airports.

The AER undertakes a number of roles in the energy. It remains financially a part of the ACCC for government reporting requirements although operating with separate program funding.[2] Under the Australian model agencies and government departments are funded on a program basis. This is explained further under the section on the Portfolio Budget Statements below.

Commissioners of the ACCC are appointed by the government (through the Governor-General) for a period of no more than five years, but are eligible for re-appointment. There are seven Commissioners and four Associate Commissioners, including the Chairperson. All are appointed on the basis of their knowledge and/or experience in industry, commerce, economics, law, and public administration or consumer protection. At least one member must be a person with knowledge of, or experience in, consumer protection and one in small business.

State and Territory governments are consulted on membership and a simple majority (including the Commonwealth) is required for recommending appointment by the government of the day through the Governor-General.

The ACCC Commissioners meet weekly to make formal decisions. The ACCC has two types of committees: subject matter committees, which help the Commission in its decision-making and other functions, and corporate governance committees. Subject matter committees include the Merger Review Committee, the Authorisation Committee, the Enforcement Committee, the Infrastructure Committee and the Communications Committee. Statutory decisions are made by the full Commission following consideration by the subject matter committees. For the purposes of this case study, the subject matter committee is the Communications Committee which meets fortnightly to consider telecommunications industry regulatory issues and refers recommendations to the full Commission for decision. The Communications Committee is comprised of four members of the Commission but doesn't have statutory decision making power

The AER Board is the relevant decision maker in the energy sector. The Australian Energy Market Agreement states that the appointment of Board members to the AER will be in accordance with the CCA. The Board consists of 3 members, two of whom are to be recommended for appointment by agreement of at least five of the COAG Ministers representing each of the States and Territories that have elected to be subject to the jurisdiction of the AER and the third to be recommended for appointment by the Chair of the ACCC ("Commonwealth AER Member"). Provision may be made for the appointment of acting Members on the same basis. The Board of the AER meets weekly.

## Reform agenda: Commonwealth governance measures

### *Performance assessment and reporting*

*The Commonwealth Resource Management Framework* [3] relates to how the Commonwealth of Australia uses and manages its resources. The framework is an important feature of an accountable and transparent public sector and informs the Australian people of the daily work of Commonwealth entities, accountable authorities and their employees. The framework is based on the *Public Governance, Performance and Accountability Act 2013* (PGPA Act) and is supported by suite of rules, policy and guidance. The Act took effect on 1 July 2014.

Two current governance reform programmes being implemented by the Australian Commonwealth Government (the Commonwealth) are of particular relevance to the issues of accountability and transparency. The Commonwealth Performance Framework (CPF) is a broad based program aimed at all government departments and agencies while the Regulator Performance Framework (RPF) is aimed at regulators only. The programs are both based in large part on calls from government and other stakeholders for increased accountability and transparency in the operations of government entities.

The ACCC is subject to both performance frameworks. In recognition of specific accountability framework already operating under the CoAG Energy Council – which is consistent with the RPF – the AER is subject only to the CPF.

### *The Regulator Performance Framework (RPF)*

On 30 October 2014, the Australian government released its final Regulatory Performance Framework (RPF). The RPF establishes a common set of performance measures that will allow for the assessment of regulators' performance and their engagement with stakeholders. All Commonwealth regulators will be assessed against six key performance indicators (KPIs):

- regulators do not unnecessarily impede the efficient operation of regulated entities;
- communication with regulated entities is clear, targeted and effective;
- actions taken by regulators are proportionate to the risk being managed;

- compliance and monitoring approaches are streamlined and co-ordinated;
- regulators are open and transparent in their dealings with regulated entities; and
- regulators actively contribute to the continuous improvement of regulatory frameworks.

These frameworks are designed to complement each other, not to operate as separate, parallel processes, nor to completely overlap. They are important in the context of accountability and transparency as they are intended to improve on these principles to provide government, industry and the public with a better understanding of the performance of regulators and agencies. While basically externally focused they also have the potential to provide substantial information to management to help improve operational performance.

The case studies on accountability and transparency demonstrate the importance of the wide range of measures and tools for management. They provide metrics to measure performance for internal use, not just for external stakeholders, while also delivering on a framework that imposes strong discipline by calling management to account in meeting their objectives and performance measures.

There are a number of recurring themes across these frameworks. These relate to how regulators should approach measuring and reporting their performance in order to ensure that accountability metrics truly reflect performance and that all stakeholders and interested parties are able to access and understand all relevant information and to make judgements accordingly. These include:

- clearly defining a set of indicators of good performance that are relevant to the regulator's specific responsibilities and activities – this process should involve stakeholder input;
- identifying appropriate data and information that can be used to measure performance against the indicators;
- conducting regular audits/assessments of performance against the indicators – this should include structured feedback from stakeholders subject to the regulation; and
- publishing findings in a public forum, such as on the regulator's website.

These themes are clearly related to regulatory accountability and the transparency and appropriateness of reporting and measures to underpin the accountability. The RPF aims to provide some assurance to stakeholders that regulators are cognisant of the costs they may impose on regulated entities and that they are actively applying measures to either limit the costs of compliance or make it clear to the market what those costs are and the trade-offs involved in terms of cost-benefit.

### The Commonwealth Performance Framework (CPF)

The second stage of the PGPA Act reforms focuses on the introduction and implementation of the Commonwealth Performance Framework (CPF). The purpose of the framework is to provide a clear link between the resourcing, planning, results and reporting activities of an agency to support more effective government operations and more efficient decision making about the allocation of scarce resources. That is, to ensure accountability and to develop quantitative and qualitative metrics that provides the agency and/or the regulator and interested observers with sufficient information to assess the entity's performance and to drive operational change.

The emphasis is on the development and use of improved key performance measures. The measures are both quantitative and qualitative with recognition on the part of policy makers that a robust set of measures may take some time given the current position. The importance of qualitative performance reporting including evaluations, reviews, surveys and other forms of measurement tools and approaches has been recognised as integral in the assessment of outcome performance in government entities over time.[4]

## Accountability and transparency: ACCC and AER frameworks

### Accountability to a minister and the legislature

The AER and the ACCC are independent decision making bodies with their independence guaranteed by legislation. It is well accepted that independence requires strong accountability measures given the powers and impact an independent regulator has. The ACCC and the AER are both formally accountable through Ministers to Parliament and through various permanent and ad hoc Committees. This ensures that the two bodies are subject to formal public oversight in order that they may be held accountable for their actions and activities.

As noted above, the AER has no separate financial identity although it does have a specific program under the ACCC's budget that allows interested parties to hold both the ACCC and the AER accountable for the resources provided by the government. AER focused reporting that underpins greater transparency to stakeholders and interested parties is discussed in the section below on the AER.

The Senate has a long established practice consisting of various committees that consider Departmental and Agency expenditure through what is known as Senate Estimates. The opportunity to examine the operations of government plays a key role in the Parliamentary scrutiny (i.e. accountability) of the executive. There are also ad hoc Parliamentary Committees to which the executive may be called to give evidence on particular issues of relevance to the ACCC and AER areas of expertise or operations.

In addition to Parliamentary accountability both bodies' decisions may be subject to legal challenge through the courts and/or competition tribunals. This reflects another key aspect of formal accountability in that decisions of the independent regulator can in turn be appealed to an independent judicial body, or semi-judicial in the case of the Australian Competition Tribunal (ACT). This is a cornerstone of accountability and helps to underpin acceptance of a regulator's independent status. It also addresses some of the concerns that are occasionally raised around the fact that the regulator is an unelected body making decisions impacting on the rights of citizens.

## *Portfolio Budget Statement (PBS)*

The PBS plays a key role in the formal accountability framework through informing Parliament and the public of the allocation of resources to departments and their relevant portfolio agencies. PBSs, together with the Budget Papers, are publicly available documents which explain the government's budget decisions. They also provide further information (financial and non-financial) at the Portfolio and agency level about the on-going policy and programme delivery initiatives of the government.

The PBS identifies resourcing decisions of government and links these to the strategic direction of the relevant agency and then to a set of key program deliverables. It is, therefore, a primary mechanisms by which the executive government remains accountable to the Parliament and the public. Taken together with corporate plans, annual reports and annual performance statements, an interested observer is able to gather evidence as to how resources are being directed towards the outcomes identified in the various statements.

It is within this framework that the AER is identified as a separate program allowing observers greater transparency in regard to the resourcing of the energy regulatory functions. The PBS is the basis for the estimates hearings noted above as they allow Parliamentary members to question the expenditure noted in the statements.

## *Corporate Plan*

The ACCC and AER Corporate Plan sets out the purpose and goals and the strategies to be pursued in the coming financial year to achieve those goals. It also sets out the actions the ACCC and AER will take under those strategies. It is important to understand that the Corporate Plan brings together information and goals, strategies and measures that provide an interested party with a broad view of the total agency resourcing, strategies and future planning. The AER also has a more developed plan that is built into its Statement of Expectations (SoE) to the Council of Australian Governments Energy Council (COAG EC) and allows a much deeper and detailed assessment of the energy regulator's plans in regard to its operations.

The Corporate Plan sets out the core goals of the ACCC and the AER. Under each goal is a set of strategies and measures to evaluate those strategies.[5] These are then reported on in the Annual Report to allow readers to assess whether or not the regulators are actually achieving their stated goals.

## *Annual Report*

The Annual Report is a basic accountability building block for all government departments and agencies. The ACCC and AER in accordance with section 63 of the Public Service Act 1999 produce an annual report each year. The report sets out the actions taken to achieve the goals listed in the Corporate Plan over the past year. The AER also produces an additional annual report, setting out how it has addressed its Statement of Intent and KPIs.

Annual Reports provide a high degree of visibility in terms of financial accountability in particular but also in ensuring agencies/departments provide information on their operations. For example the ACCC and AER Annual reports provide snapshots of their financial position in addition to the more explicit and audited financial statements.

The report provides information on cases litigated and their outcomes, undertakings accepted, infringement notices paid, use of agency coercive powers, mergers etc. encompassing a raft of statistics and regulatory decisions made.

A requirement of the CPF is that the ACCC and AER must report on progress against performance measures identified in the Corporate Plan at the start of the financial year. This reporting is contained in an annual performance statement, which has replaced the performance section that has previously been included in Commonwealth entities' annual reports. The requirements for annual performance statements are designed to provide a consistent approach to performance reporting across all entities.

The Australian National Audit Office (ANAO) plays an important role in overseeing the formal measures. It is the mandated auditor, ensuring the financial accounts are correct and also undertakes various programme reviews across the public sector.

## *Statement of Expectations*

The Australian government's SoE outlines its expectations about the role and responsibilities of the ACCC, its relationship with the government, issues of transparency and accountability and operational matters. It forms part of the government's commitment to good corporate governance of agencies and reducing the regulatory burden on business and the community.

The AER's Statement of Expectations focuses on its particular areas of responsibility (the AER SoE/SoI will be further considered in the section relating solely to the AER's accountability and transparency measures).

The SoE applies to the whole of ACCC and outlines the government's expectations in regard to the manner in which the ACCC operates in performance of its roles and responsibilities. Similarly, the AER's SoE references its roles and responsibilities. The SoEs direct the ACCC and AER to undertake their activities in accordance with regulatory best practice in decision making, policy development, operational practices and communications.

## *Statement of Intent*

The ACCC notes in its SoI that while it is an independent statutory authority it is important for it to take into account the government's broad policy framework in performance of its roles and responsibilities.

The ACCC commits to providing timely and accurate information to Treasury Portfolio Ministers, subject to the ACCC's obligations regarding the protection of investigative information. The Chairperson will meet regularly with the ACCC's responsible Minister and/or his office to provide updates on ACCC activities and matters of significance to the government, and other ministers as required. The ACCC (and the AER in its SoI) also commit to ensuring that best practice is employed in its regulatory practices and that the regulator commits to assessing the compliance costs of its action.

These measures represent the more formal accountability framework mandated through government policy and/or legislation. However, they are also important in what they offer business and the public in that they provide a rich vein of information that can be accessed at various levels of complexity to both inform and guide.

## Section B: ACCC telecommunications regulatory framework

As noted above, the ACCC has a range of regulatory functions in relation to national infrastructure industries as well as a prices oversight role in some markets where competition is limited. The ACCC's functions include:

- determining the prices and access terms and conditions for some nationally significant infrastructure services

- monitoring and enforcing compliance with industry-specific laws for bulk water, energy and communications

- monitoring and reporting on prices and quality of particular goods and services to provide information about the effects of market conditions

- disseminating information to help stakeholders understand regulatory frameworks and the structure and operation of infrastructure markets

- providing advice when requested by governments and policy agencies on how efficient regulatory outcomes and competitive, well-functioning markets can be achieved.

Part XIB and XIC of the CCA are the communications industry-specific provisions of the CCA. Telecommunications markets in Australia were opened to full competition in 1997 and responsibility for the economic and competition regulation of the industry was passed to the ACCC. The ACCC's role under the Competition and Consumer Act 2010 (CCA) is to promote competition and efficient investment in this and other regulated industries, including electricity, gas and aviation.

The principal barrier to competition in network industries such as telecommunications is that they rely on facilities that are not easy or economic to duplicate. Therefore, a right of access is provided for competitors wishing to use these facilities. The task is to ensure fair prices and non-price conditions of access for the benefit of wholesale users, while encouraging adequate investment in new facilities.

The ACCC administers the telecommunications specific provisions in the CCA, comprising the competitive safeguards contained in Part XIB, and the access regime contained in Part XIC. Significant amendments to the industry-specific provisions were passed by Parliament in late 2010 to streamline access arrangements and address industry structure issues

The ACCC has additional communications-specific responsibilities under the following national legislation: Broadcasting Services Act 1992; Copyright Act 1968; National Broadband Network Companies Act 2011; Radiocommunications Act 1992; Telecommunications (Consumer Protection Services Standards) Act 1999; and the Telecommunications Act 1997.

## *Objectives*

The core objectives of the ACCC's communications function, which is a part of the broader Infrastructure Regulation Division, are to:

- deliver network regulation to promote competition and meet the long-term interests of end users.
- improve the workability of emerging markets by enforcing market rules and monitoring market outcomes.

## *Access regulation*

Part XIC of the CCA supports the development of a competitive telecommunications industry by allowing services to be 'declared', a process that determines which services are regulated by the ACCC. Once declared, a service must be supplied, on request, to other providers for use in their own services. This arrangement guarantees access to telecommunications services in the interest of competitive services to end-users.

In regulating the telecommunications sector, the ACCC aims to establish reasonable access terms that:

- balance the interests of infrastructure owners, users and the broader public
- achieve any-to-any connectivity
- encourage efficient investment in, and use of, infrastructure promote competition for the long-term benefit of consumers and businesses.

### Introduction of a new wholesale access network

On 13 December 2013, the ACCC accepted the varied special access undertaking (SAU) lodged by the National Broadband Network Co (NBN) on 19 November 2013. The NBN is an entity owned by the Australian government and tasked with developing a national, open-access broadband network. The SAU, which will operate until June 2040, includes terms and conditions for access to the national network and sets the broad regulatory framework for effective engagement between NBN Co and access seekers to negotiate commercial agreements.

Telstra's (the current monopoly network provider) Structural Separation Undertaking (SSU) also includes commitments to safeguard competition until the NBN is built and Telstra has migrated its fixed line services to the new network. Of particular significance is Telstra's commitment to providing equivalent service levels to wholesale customers and its own retail businesses.

### Anti-competitive conduct

Part XIB applies certain general anti-competitive conduct provisions of part IV of the CCA to telecommunications carriers and carriage service providers (CSPs) via the 'competition rule'. A carrier or CSP may breach the competition rule if it contravenes certain provisions of part IV in respect of a telecommunications market.

A carrier or CSP may also breach the competition rule if it has a substantial degree of market power in a telecommunications market and takes advantage of that power with the effect, or likely effect, of substantially lessening competition in any telecommunications market, or takes advantage of that power and engages in other conduct and the combined effect, or likely effect, is to substantially lessen competition in any telecommunications market.

## Functions and powers

### Declaration and access conditions for communications services

The ACCC can declare a service by:

- holding a public inquiry and allowing access providers, access seekers and consumers to comment; or
- accepting a special access undertaking from the provider of a service which effectively declares a particular service.

Once a service has been declared, the ACCC must make final access determinations for all services that it declares. These determinations enable the ACCC to set default price and non-price terms for declared services. The terms only apply where there is no commercial agreement between an access seeker and an access provider, creating a benchmark which access seekers can fall back on while still allowing parties to negotiate different terms.

## *Oversight of Telstra's structural separation*

As part of the ACCC's role in ensuring a smooth transition to the NBN, it oversees Telstra's SSU and migration plan. Together these outline how Telstra will progressively stop supplying telephone and broadband services over its copper and hybrid fibre coaxial (HFC) networks and migrate those services to the NBN. Each financial year the ACCC must monitor and report to the Minister for Communication on Telstra's breaches, if any, of its structural separation undertaking and migration plan.

## *Industry-specific codes and rules*

The ACCC is also involved in reviewing and overseeing a number of industry-specific codes and rules. On 4 July 2012, the ACCC began a review of the Facilities Access Code following changes to the Telecommunications Act 1997 and the CCA. The Facilities Access Code sets out arrangements for carriers wishing to install their equipment on or in facilities owned by other carriers. The facilities covered by the code include telecommunications transmission towers, the tower sites, and underground facilities designed to hold lines.

The ACCC consulted on a draft decision to vary the code in May 2013. In September 2013, the ACCC decided to vary the code to remove obsolete references, reflect legislative changes and align it with Telstra's SSU.

## *Statutory reporting*

The ACCC collects a range of information from telecommunications companies to monitor competition, market developments and inform its decisions. The Minister can also require the ACCC to monitor and report on various aspects of competition within the industry. In addition, the ACCC reports to the Minster on Telstra's compliance with retail price controls imposed by the Minister.

In response to statutory reporting requirements, the ACCC released the following reports in 2013 14, all of which are available on the ACCC website:

- ACCC Telecommunications Report 2012–13
- Telstra's compliance with retail price control arrangements 2012–13
- Telstra's Structural Separation Undertaking – Compliance Report 2012–13
- NBN points of interconnection: Review of policies and procedures relating to the identification of listed points of interconnection to the NBN

The ACCC's involvement in the sector includes:

- Access regulation which aims to:
    - balance the interests of infrastructure owners, users and the broader public
    - achieve any-to-any connectivity
    - encourage efficient investment in, and use of, infrastructure promote competition for the long-term benefit of consumers and businesses.
- Introduction of a new wholesale access network:
    - agree and oversee the SAU as part of fundamental changes to the Australian Telecommunications sector
    - agree and oversee structural separation arrangements in regard to the former monopoly incumbent and current major market player (Telstra).
- Investigation of telecommunications specific anti-competitive conduct and assist ACCC Enforcement Division in consumer protection investigations and litigation

## Accountability to a minister and the legislature

The ACCC, in its telecommunications role, has the same accountability requirements as identified in the first section, that is, accountability to the Parliament through the appropriate minister. There is a slight complication in the case of the telecommunications area as there is another minister involved in telecommunications issues (Minister for Communications and Broadband). However, the formal requirements remain as stated with no additional requirements imposed due to the involvement of an additional minister.

There is however, a stakeholder engagement imperative whereby the ACCC takes action to inform the minister of impending decisions that may impact on his/her portfolio.

## Accountability to regulated entities

### *Consultation*

It is standard practice for the ACCC to conduct multi-stage, public consultation processes as a cornerstone of its regulatory processes. These processes usually entail publishing a discussion paper on the ACCC website that regulated entities and affected parties can respond to. After reviewing submissions, the ACCC will then further consider its position on the matter and release a draft decision. Following another round of submissions to the draft decision, the ACCC will issue its final decision.

The ACCC has also begun to experiment with forums that involve all sides to a particular issue and in which various suggestions and differing views are aired with the involvement of senior ACCC staff and relevant Commissioners. This was a highly useful tool in the assessment of the NBN undertaking and the range of matters that concerned the industry, lobby groups (such as consumer groups) and NBN itself. This may become a business as usual tool for the ACCC communications area in future matters.

### *Infrastructure Consultative Committee*

The Infrastructure Consultative Committee was set up in 2006 to facilitate discussions on the broad issues of infrastructure and infrastructure regulation. The committee was selected to be representative of the diversity of infrastructure interests and includes representatives from energy, telecommunication, water, rail, ports, and airports. This committee also fits well with the overall ACCC commitment to transparency encouraging greater visibility across the various infrastructure sectors and demonstrating the ACCC's regulatory approach and broader philosophy of economic regulation.

The committee is an important mechanism for the ACCC to gain feedback from stakeholders in the infrastructure sector. Operational issues and the specifics of decisions that are before the ACCC and AER are not the focus of this committee. Rather, the emphasis is on issues in the practice of regulation that cross the different infrastructure sectors.

## Wholesale Telecommunications Consultative Forum

The Wholesale Telecommunications Consultative Forum was established in 2012 to provide an opportunity for meaningful dialogue between the ACCC and the telecommunications industry. It also provides information to increase the ACCC's understanding of structural separation and migration issues and to assist the ACCC in undertaking its roles under the CCA and Telecommunications Act 1997. A range of wholesale telecommunications industry participants and other interested parties have been invited to the forum to ensure a wide range of relevant views are represented.

### Accountability to the public

Many of the tools and mechanisms reported above are useful to the public in providing reports on the work of the ACCC's communications area and giving the public the opportunity to make informed assessments of the regulator's performance. Importantly, the fact that these processes are available on the ACCC web site (and directly through a set of contacts and interested persons that has grown over time) means that there is a greater likelihood of involvement in the various regulatory processes from a wider group of stakeholders. It also means that the regulatory processes and associated decisions are better understood and that criticism if forthcoming is based on a better appreciation of the issues.

The ACCC has prepared a number of fact sheets for consumers that describe in simple, non-technical language how the ACCC sets rules for the supply of telecommunications services: www.accc.gov.au/regulated-infrastructure/communications/accc-role-in-communications/consumer-fact-sheets-for-telecommunications-services.

This is an important element of the ACCC's efforts to inform the public more broadly of its role in the telecommunications sector. In terms of transparency it allows the general public to gain much greater clarity into the complex world of telecommunications services and markets. As with the Office of Rail Regulation in the United Kingdom this practice helps to encourage a more educated consumer cohort able to call service providers as well as the regulator to account and to provide better informed input into regulatory processes.

## Transparency

The ACCC publishes the latest regulatory reports, determinations and issues papers on its website along with up-to-date information on ongoing processes such as:

- the ACCC's final determination of NBN Co's Special Access Undertaking
- implementation of Telstra's Structural Separation Undertaking and migration plan, including implementation of the independent telecommunications adjudicator scheme
- access determination inquiries
- lodgement of access agreements by carriers or carriage service providers relating to access to a regulated service.

These papers help inform stakeholders about key industry developments and current consultations. The ACCC Telecommunications Report is an annual report that provides an in-depth view on the telecommunications sector and its various services and products. It takes a particular position in informing readers on the competitive developments in the sector to give a year on year assessment of the progress of the markets.

The Accountability and Transparency section in the introduction to the ORR case study noted the diversity of parties with an interest in the performance of the regulators. This diversity in turn requires a range of transparency measures to satisfy the demands of the various actors, both in depth of information and complexity. The set of formal and informal measures cannot be viewed in isolation. Each measure should complement the other and the extent to which they are implemented will reflect the cultural commitment of the regulators' senior management to a fully transparent approach to its duties and practices.

Formal requirements provide confidence to Ministers, Parliament and relevant central treasury and finance departments as to the performance of the ACCC in responding to policy imperatives and its stewardship of taxpayer funds. These measures also allow interested observers to put together a full picture of the ACCC's communications role operations and its impact on the market.

The formal PBS, SoE/SoI, corporate plan and annual reports and Senate Committees, work hand in hand with the ACCC processes around consultation, public process, a web site in which is information rich, and a willingness of the regulator to develop, implement and report on its KPIs.

One of the important and sometimes underrated tools available to regulators, and noted in the NER PAFER pilot and the ORR case study, is to publish well researched reports on the broader market, not just on specific regulatory decisions. The ACCC's telecommunications report continues this theme. While the reports are not directly related to statutory decisions, or obviously part of the individual suite of accountability and transparency measures, they do give observers a clear, year on year picture of the market. This allows much better informed judgments as to the impact or otherwise of the regulatory regime in either aiding or restricting the development of competitive markets.

## Section C: AER regulatory framework

The Australian Energy Regulator (AER) is an independent entity under the Competition and Consumer Act 2010 (CCA), consisting of two state/territory members and one Commonwealth member. The CCA sets out the process for appointing AER Board members and making decisions.

The AER's functions are set out in the national energy legislation and rules, which include the National Electricity Law, the National Gas Law and the National Energy Retail Law. The Australian Energy Market Agreement 2004 sets out the co-operative legislative framework of the states/territories and the Commonwealth. South Australia is the lead legislator, and the other jurisdictions then apply the national energy legislation. Independence in its decision-making is guaranteed under the enabling legislation.

### *Objectives*

The AER's core objective is to maintain and promote competition in wholesale energy markets;

- build consumer confidence in energy markets;
- promote efficient investment in, operation and use of, energy networks and services for the long-term interests of consumers; and
- strengthen stakeholder engagement in energy markets and regulatory processes.

### *Functions and powers*

The AER regulates energy markets and networks under national energy market legislation and rules. Its core functions, which mostly relate to energy markets in eastern and southern Australia, include:

- setting the prices charged for using energy networks (electricity poles and wires and gas pipelines) to transport energy to customers;
- monitoring wholesale electricity and gas markets to ensure suppliers comply with the legislation and rules, and taking enforcement action where necessary;
- regulating retail energy markets in the ACT, Queensland, South Australia, Tasmania (electricity only) and New South Wales. This includes enforcing compliance with retail legislation; authorising retailers to sell energy; approving retailers' policies for dealing with customers in hardship; administering a national retailer of last resort scheme; reporting on retailer performance; educating consumers and small businesses about their energy rights; and managing the energy price comparison website – Energy Made Easy;
- publishing information on energy markets, including the annual State of the energy market report and more detailed market and compliance reporting, to assist participants and the wider community.

In addition, the AER assists the ACCC with energy related issues arising under the CCA, including enforcement, mergers and adjudication.

*Reform agenda*

In addition to the broader governance reform agenda noted above, over 2012 there were reviews across the full spectrum of energy regulation. These included:

- a wholesale review of the rules that set out how network prices are determined, which was initiated by the rule changes lodged by the AER;
- a review of the effectiveness of the process for reviewing the AER's regulatory decisions;
- a review of the effectiveness of the Australian Competition Tribunal as the review body;
- reviews of how reliability standards are set;
- reviews of how the demand side can be better incorporated into the market; and
- a range of reviews considering how the long term interests of consumers can be better integrated with the regulatory process.

On 15 November 2012, the Australian Energy Market Commission (AEMC) made a final determination on new rules to regulate electricity network prices.

The new rules better equip the AER to develop methods and processes to achieve efficient outcomes in setting revenues and prices for consumers in a number of areas. They include how the rate of return on capital is set.

The new National Electricity Rules mean the AER is able to adapt its approaches to the nature of the business it is regulating. They clarify the AER's powers to undertake benchmarking, including requiring the regulator to publish annual reports on the relative efficiencies of electricity network businesses. The new rules aim to promote greater confidence in regulatory outcomes through improved operational effectiveness.

This enhanced framework comes hand in hand with a renewed emphasis on and commitment from the AER to its accountability. This is evident in improved reporting in regards to its strategic and operational plans and performance against a well-developed and institutionalised set of KPIs.

On 7 December 2012, the COAG endorsed a comprehensive package of national energy market reforms developed collaboratively by the Standing Council on Energy and Resources (SCER) to respond to the challenges of rising electricity prices.

The package of reforms aimed to restore the focus of the electricity market on serving the long term interests of consumers and was built around four key themes:

- strengthening regulation;
- empowering consumers;
- enhancing competition and innovations; and
- ensuring balanced network investment.

## *Better Regulation programme*

The AER's Better Regulation programme aimed to deliver an improved regulatory framework focused on promoting the long term interests of electricity consumers. This followed from changes to the National Electricity and Gas Rules that were published by the Australian Energy Market Commission on 29 November 2012.

As part of the Better Regulation programme the AER:

- Published a series of guidelines in November and December 2013 which set out the AER's approach to regulation under the new rules.

- Established a Consumer Reference Group to make it easier for consumer representative groups to have input into the Better regulation consultative process without necessarily writing formal submissions.
- Established a Consumer Challenge Panel within the AER on 1 July 2013. The Panel provides an independent consumer perspective to challenge the AER and network service providers during determination processes.

## *Accountability and transparency*

### *Accountability to a minister and the legislature*

#### COAG arrangements

The following discussion relates to accountability and transparency mechanisms beyond those noted above in the general discussion of the ACCC and AER.

The Council of Australian Governments (COAG) Energy Council is responsible for major energy reform and the national energy legislation. The council consists of the Commonwealth, State, Territory and New Zealand energy and resources ministers.

The AER reports biannually to the ministers on work activities, key market outcomes and, if requested, its views on reform proposals. The AER Chair and CEO usually attend part of each COAG Energy Council meeting to discuss energy market and network regulation issues.

The COAG Energy Council in March 2014 outlined what it expects from the AER under new accountability and performance frameworks. In response, the AER in June 2014 published its inaugural Statement of Intent, setting out how it will meet those expectations during 2014-15, including through its strategic priorities and wider ongoing work programme. The statement also sets out deliverables and performance indicators to measure the AER's progress in meeting expectations.

These deliverables and performance indicators are reported on in the AER Annual Report, which provides all interested parties the opportunity to assess regulatory performance, including where measures aren't met and performance has suffered.

Portfolio budget statements and corporate plans

As noted above, each year, as part of the Commonwealth Budget, the Portfolio Budget Statement: Treasury Portfolio budget papers sets out programme deliverables and performance indicators for the AER. From the portfolio budget statement, an AER and ACCC corporate plan is developed. The AER then develop an internal business plan that reflects the corporate plan and the portfolio budget statement. It contains a risk matrix to help the AER minimise risks. This plan is public and has strong links to the SoE.

## *Accountability to regulated entities*

### *Consultation*

The AER expressly aims to avoid a regulatory approach based solely on an iterative 'documentation exchange'. Instead, it wants to focus more on inquiry, questioning and understanding. To strengthen accountability to regulated entities in day to day dealings the AER have relationship managers at the Director level to handle communication with each business, and to facilitate communication between the business and staff. Regulated businesses can also present key aspects of their proposals to the AER Board, a development that has helped to ensure regulated businesses have their views heard by the decision makers.

Given the nature of the AER's role in wholesale and retail energy markets, the AER regularly contacts generators, energy retailers and other energy businesses. This includes formal, issue specific contact, as well as informal, relationship building contact.

When undertaking regulatory decisions, it is standard practice for the AER to conduct multi-stage, public consultation processes. These processes usually entail publishing a discussion paper on the AER website that regulated entities can respond to. After reviewing submissions, the AER will then further consider its position on the matter and release a draft decision. Following another round of submissions to the draft decision, the AER will issue its final decision.

### *Judicial review*

Network businesses can seek a merits review of AER decisions by the Australian Competition Tribunal. If the Tribunal reviews a network pricing decision, the AER are a party to the review. The AER must act as a model litigant, using its best endeavours to help the Tribunal make its decision. The Tribunal can remit a regulatory decision (or aspects of a decision) to the

AER for further consideration. Further, the courts can review the AER's decisions on administrative grounds.

## *Accountability to the public*

Recent energy policy reforms and review recommendations identified ways for the AER to engage more productively with energy consumers and businesses. This improvement is vital; a lack of consumer engagement in network pricing decisions makes it difficult for the AER to assess whether network business proposals reflect the services consumers want. More generally, an imbalance in the views reflected in regulatory decisions can reduce consumer confidence in the energy market, its regulation and its outcomes.

The regulatory framework with the network businesses' proposals is complex, which can limit consumer engagement in network decisions. Consumer representative organisations highlighted their need for significant resources and specialist skills to contribute meaningfully to the AER's regulatory reviews. This problem was recognised in recent reforms to the energy rules, and in reviews by the Merits Review Expert Panel, the Senate Select Committee and the Productivity Commission.

The reviews identified value in stronger consumer involvement in determining how energy businesses are regulated, and in undertaking regulatory processes. So, the reforms target more constructive approaches for the AER and energy businesses to engage with consumers. In response, the AER introduced several initiatives to increase consumer participation in the energy sector and AER processes:

- established a Consumer Reference Group as part of the Better Regulation programme so consumer representatives could more meaningfully participate in the process;
- developed a service provider consumer engagement guideline to help network businesses deliver on their new obligations to engage with consumers when developing their regulatory proposals;
- introduced a Consumer Challenge Panel to help incorporate consumers' interests in decisions on the prices energy network businesses charged; and
- used the Customer Consultative Group to help understand consumer perspectives on retail energy market issues.

The Consumer Challenge Panel and Customer Consultative Group complement wider initiatives aimed at empowering consumers. The COAG Energy Council has established a national energy consumer advocacy body,

Energy Consumers Australia. The consumer advocate will engage with consumers and build expertise and capacity on issues that advance energy consumers' interests. It will also manage and fund grants for research to engage and influence policy development and consumer education in the markets.

*Transparency*

As with telecommunications and the ORR's transparency framework (for which, see the case study below) many of the accountability mechanisms discussed above in reference to both the ACCC and AER are fundamental in assuring transparency. Annual reports, corporate plans and especially for the AER its SoI are all extremely important transparency mechanisms.

The SoI in particular provides substantial information on the proposed work programme and when read in conjunction with the AER's annual report allows a reader to draw conclusions as to the success or otherwise of the AER in meeting its goals. This is a powerful tool both in terms of holding the regulator to account but also in ensuring that there is a high degree of discipline imposed on the regulator to meet its commitments.

The AER is clear in informing its stakeholders through these reports of its challenges and any gaps in achieving the tasks it has set itself.

*AER Stakeholder Engagement Strategy*

The AER Stakeholder Engagement Strategy is an important additional element of the AER's accountability and transparency framework. The strategy was specifically designed and implemented in recognition that the decisions the AER makes and the actions taken in performing its regulatory roles and other activities, affect a wide range of individuals, businesses and organisations

The Stakeholder Engagement Framework works towards ensuring all stakeholders have the opportunity to engage and thereby build trust in the regulators' decision making by providing a structure that allows stakeholders' needs and interests to be consistently, transparently and meaningfully considered.

The core objectives are based around building strong and effective communication channels and facilitating understanding by the stakeholders, especially by enhancing the clarity, accessibility, relevance and timeliness of communication. However, the framework also plays a role in accountability through the commitment to stakeholders in regard to the provision of and access to proper information. The Engagement Framework sets out a set of principles that underpin its commitment to its stakeholders. The fact that these are published, reported on with a commitment to measure engagement provides a strong discipline on the AER, complementing the range of accountability mechanisms already identified:

- Principle 1: Clear, accurate and timely communication
- Principle 2: Accessible and inclusive
- Principle 3: Transparent
- Principle 4: Measurable

AER also commits to reviewing and evaluating the performance against the above principles and, if necessary, amending and adding to this document. The AER also commits to reporting publicly on any review following consultation with stakeholders.

*Stakeholder survey*

Stakeholder surveys are a useful tool to seek feedback on performance. When results are also published they greatly reinforce the picture of an accountable and responsive regulator. Surveying a broad range of stakeholders and publishing the results is helpful in promoting transparency and good governance, including accountability.

The AER periodically survey external stakeholders and publish the results on its website. These surveys of consumer representatives, the businesses the AER regulates, other energy bodies, departments and ministers, focus on the AER's performance, consultation, reputation and communication. The ratings empirically measure how the AER meets a set of key performance indicators. The results provide highly relevant and useful input to the AER's planning and operational processes and also allow the agency to clarify how it is viewed in terms of its work in developing its strategic priorities and approach to stakeholder engagement.

These feedback loops are important for both regulator and regulatory observers in that they provide strong basis for decision making and for assessing perceptions as to the effectiveness or otherwise of the regulator. Care must always be taken in interpreting surveys, and particular in considering whether negative commentary or sentiment is a result of poor practices or the more mundane dislike of what are otherwise strong regulatory decisions.

The first set of questions in the survey is about the AER's overall performance. They go to the key capabilities of a good regulatory agency, such as impartiality, transparency and timeliness of decisions. The survey then seeks more specific feedback on three areas of performance, namely engagement, communication and technical capability.

*Performance indicators*

The AER includes a chapter in its Annual Report that reports on organisational performance against a comprehensive set of target deliverables. For each indicator, the AER includes a "traffic light report" – a green light indicates achievement of the performance target, and light green and dark grey lights indicate failure to fully achieve. Where the AER does not meet a performance target, it explains why. And, in some instances, outlines measures to improve performance.

In addition to quantitative targets the AER has a range of qualitative measures that it reports on. Like many other successful regulators the AER takes considerable time and effort in explaining the actions it undertakes through well written case studies and stories relating to its operations.

The performance indicators are set around each of the strategic priorities in the AER's forward plan. Currently these are:

- The Better Regulation programme
- Strengthening stakeholder engagement
- Building confidence in markets
- Improving internal capabilities

For example, the indicators for the Better Regulation Program include publishing a specific number of guidelines; preparation of clear consultation documents clearly identifying stakeholder views and the AER's response to them; internal review of effectiveness in delivering the program; engage with regulated business to ensure compliance with the program as evidenced by engagement processes, forums etc. Each objective is similarly assessed through a number of indicators with results published and if necessary opens to examination and assessment by third parties.

# Notes

1. Government of Australia (2005), "Treasury Portfolio Budget Statement 2005-2006), www:budget.gov.au/2005-06/pbs/html/index_tsy.htm.
2. See Appendix A for a short note on challenges arising from the ACCC/AER institutional model.
3. www.finance.gov.au/resource-management.
4. Note the similarities and links to the NER's PAFER (see OECD, 2015c).
5. ACCC and AER Corporate Plan 2014-15.

## Bibliography

ACCC and AER (2015), "Corporate Plan and Priorities 2015-16", https://www.accc.gov.au/publications/corporate-plan-priorities/corporate-plan-priorities-2015-16 (accessed 24 July 2015).

ACCC and AER (2014), "Annual Report 2013-14", https://www.accc.gov.au/publications/accc-aer-annual-report/accc-aer-annual-report-2013-14 (accessed 24 July 2015).

ACCC (n.d.), "The Australian Competition & Consumer Commission's accountability framework for investigations", https://www.accc.gov.au/system/files/ACCC%27s%20accountablility%20framework%20for%20investigations.pdf (accessed 24 July 2015).

Australian Government Treasury (2015), "ACCC Portfolio Budget Statement", www.treasury.gov.au/~/media/treasury/publications%20and%20media/publications/2015/pbs%202015/downloads/pdf/03_accc.ashx (accessed 24 July 2015).

Gray, H. (2013), "RAD-wide Regulatory Frameworks Jan 2011", updated May 2013, unpublished.

Pearson, M. (2011), "Australia's One Organisation Approach to Regulation and Competition Law", presented to the Multi-year expert meeting non Services, Development and Trade, UNCTAD Geneva, 6-8 April 2011.

# Chapter 4

# Portugal's Water and Waste Services Regulation Authority (ERSAR)

*This chapter presents some of the arrangements and practices related to co-ordination put in place by Portugal's Water and Waste Services Regulation Authority.*

In the early 1990's the Portuguese government undertook concerted efforts to reform the water and the waste sectors. The process of reform recognised the fundamental importance of having effective operations in the delivery of water, wastewater and municipal waste management services to the public as essential infrastructure to support ongoing economic development and to underpin the well-being of the Portuguese people.

Linking the sectors in a planning and strategic development sense is important as poorly designed and implemented wastewater operations can negate any potential improvements in the delivery of water and lead to major environmental and health problems.

The availability of these services to an acceptable level across Portugal was, and still remains, a principal target of and high priority for the country's development. Portuguese policy makers and politicians recognised the underlying natural monopoly network elements much of the drinking water and wastewater management services sector and the legal monopolies inherent in the arrangements for much of the municipal waste sector. This required the establishment of a regulatory regime and associated institutional arrangements to support the broader policy aims to prevent undue influences from undermining the policy intent.

The goals of policy makers in regard to developments in these sectors are built around ensuring delivery to and protection of consumers in the face of the natural and legal monopoly providers. The regulatory regime was designed in the context of services that are essential and indispensable to a modern economy. Policy makers also embedded equity of access and efficient delivery in building the legal and regulatory framework. These protections in recognition of consumer rights and needs have been embedded under the umbrella of maintaining the financial viability and protection of the legitimate interests of the various service providers, be they public, private, municipal or a combination thereof.

The need for the Portuguese regulator, the Water and Waste Services Regulation Authority (ERSAR), to develop strong links with other participants becomes obvious when one observes the number of players. The Public Administration may need to be involved in, or at a minimum be advised of, the regulator's operations where they may impact on the other Department's or Agency's interests. These could include planning departments, finance and treasury, environmental departments and those involved in economic and regional development.

In addition there are numerous individual municipalities, associations of municipalities, inter-municipal companies, public companies, private concessions and private companies providing management services. A modern state is a highly complex organism with myriad of interactions and it is no longer possible for the various arms of the state to work in isolation. The regulatory agency cannot achieve its goals, no matter how simple, by working in a vacuum ignoring other interested parties. Arrangements need to be put in place in order to enable smooth, efficient operations, especially where there are crossovers in jurisdictional responsibilities.

---

Box 4.1. **ERSAR goals**

The fact that the water services represent natural monopolies of a local or regional basis predictably affects the competition in the sector. Due to this fact, consumers cannot choose the operator that they prefer or the price/quality relationship that they see as more convenient. Therefore, regulation has as a main goal the protection of the interests of the consumers of the services, by promoting the quality of the service provided by the operators and by ensuring the moderation of the tariffs charged by them.

However, this should be done considering the economic viability and the legitimate interests of the operators, while ensuring service sustainability in the medium and long terms. ERSAR also aims to promote other economic activities within the water and waste sector through the reinforcement of the entrepreneurial activity, as well as the contribution of these services to environmental sustainability.

Perceived as a modern tool of government intervention, the strengthening of regulation is viewed as a fundamental step for the steady growth of the sector, considering Portugal's current stage of development. The regulation is a clear sign of Portugal's transition from a phase of high infrastructure investment to a period of stabilisation and high standards of quality of service.

*Source*: ERSAR Board of Directors, www.ersar.pt/website_en/.

---

## Institutional setting

### *Sector overview*

ERSAR's scope of intervention is divided into two sectors: the water services sector and the solid waste sector. A set of overarching principles guide the policy and regulatory settings within the sectors. These principles include universal access, continuity of service, quality of service and efficient and equitable pricing. Within this structure there are two basic categories: bulk or retailing, depending on the operations of the particular sector operators.

The multi-municipal state owned systems are responsible mostly for bulk services, while the municipal systems are responsible for retail services. These correspond to the bulk and retail activities of drinking water supply, wastewater management and municipal waste management.

The water sector is in turn sub-divided into the drinking water supply, including abstraction, treatment and distribution, and wastewater management, which includes collection, transportation, treatment and disposal.

In the drinking water supply system the bulk component is located upstream from the distribution network and provides the physical connection from the water resources to the retail system. The retail system is composed of those activities and assets connected to the end-user. In some circumstances these are integrated from the upstream to the end user.

In the case of wastewater management services, municipal systems have responsibility for the retail activities, which encompass the collection and drainage of wastewater for multi-municipal systems. A bulk system includes the connection of the retail system to the point of wastewater discharge. Overall ERSAR oversees in some form or the other the operations of 400 plus operators between the various sectors.

The strategic plans for the sector have been regularly prepared and revised since 1993 with a set of strategic objectives and targets. These plans defined concrete measures to be undertaken by several actors, with an instrumental intervention of the State-owned holding "Águas de Portugal" (mainly for the bulk sector, through regional companies), of the municipalities (on the retail sector) and allowing also for private participation through concession and delegation contracts made by municipalities. Those plans have sequentially established ambitious targets to be achieved and resulted in very positive results regarding water and waste service. In the last 20 years Portugal has come from a poorly managed and substandard situation to a quite acceptable where several indicators are in line with the best in Europe. To illustrate this, some figures:

Table 4.1. **Indicators of water access and quality**

| Indicator | 1993 | 2013 |
|---|---|---|
| Access to drinking water supply through public networks | 81% | 95% |
| Drinking water quality considered safe for human consumption according to EU directives | 50% | 98% |
| Number of annual episodes of Hepatitis A (waterborne disease) | 530 | 8 |
| Access to urban wastewater management through public networks with adequate treatment | 28% | 80% |

Table 4.1. **Indicators of water access and quality** (*cont.*)

| | | |
|---|---|---|
| Quality of surface waters according to EU directives | 19% | 78% |
| Quality of coastal bathing waters according to EU directives | 55% | 99% |
| Quality of river bathing waters according to EU directives | 17% | 95% |
| Access to solid waste management with adequate treatment | 23% | 100% |
| Valorisation of solid waste | 9% | 46% |

*Source*: Information provided by ERSAR.

The third generation of strategic plans (PENSAAR 2020 and PERSU 2020) has been discussed and have been presented publicly, establishing targets for the period until 2020, mainly focused in improving the management and efficiency of water services. The projected investment for this period is around EUR 3 500 million for water and wastewater services and EUR 800 million for solid waste services.

There are two Portuguese government bodies responsible for developing and monitoring the two strategic plans for water and waste water. These are:

- ERSAR, which has responsibility for economic and quality regulation of the services and national regulation of drinking water quality; and

- the Portuguese Environment Authority (APA), which is the national water authority and the national waste authority, having a broader responsibility for environmental issues, namely water resources.

## *Legislative framework*

ERSAR is the Portuguese authority tasked with the economic and quality of service regulation of drinking water supply services, wastewater management services and municipal waste management services. It is also the national authority for drinking water quality.

Its legislative framework is substantially set around a suite of laws approved in 2009. However, the initial steps towards the current institutional framework were initiated in 1997 with Decree-Law No. 230/97 30th August and the establishment of ERSAR's predecessor, the Institute for Regulation of Water & Solid Waste (IRAR). This followed actions begun in 1993 to address structural, pricing and other strategic issues the Portuguese water supply, urban wastewater and solid waste management sectors. These reforms, among other measures, have created several regional bulk service systems responsible for the abstraction and treatment of drinking water and for the treatment and disposal of urban wastewater, and aimed at having more operational efficiency and economies of scale in terms of this service.

Decree-Law No. 243/2001 5th September extended the remit of IRAR to drinking water quality. In October 2009 the IRAR was transformed into the ERSAR through Decree-Law No. 277/2009 of 2nd October which extended the scope of the regulatory authority. This was an important step in the evolution of the regulator as it extended its regulatory oversight to all operators. Prior to 2009 the regulator did not have oversight of the operators under direct and delegated municipal management. The new regulatory framework became fully operational in August 2011. ERSAR also has full status as the national authority for drinking water through the 2001 legislation that became fully applicable 25 December 2003.

More recently Law No. 10/2014 6th March has adapted ERSAR's statutes to a new, fully independent regulation framework applied to all utilities regulators, which was established through Law No. 67/2013 of 28th August 2013. This has granted ERSAR with further independence dispositions and additional responsibilities in terms of economic regulation, especially in municipality managed services.

These reforms in regulatory laws followed a trend of adding responsibilities to the regulator both in terms of the scope of its intervention (to all operators) and of its regulatory powers. This was done following the growing recognition of the importance of regulation in solving the key structural problems of the sector, mainly in terms of its sustainability and aiming to increase quality of service.

Decree-Laws No. 362/98 of 18th November and 277/2009 of 2nd October and Law No. 10/2014 of 6th March have provided the legislative underpinning for ERSAR's establishment encompassing as they do the regulator's statutes. Due to the complexity of the market and the multi-utility natures of the regulator there is, as noted above, a suite of laws that provide the legislative backing for the regulatory arrangements.

Those not mentioned above include:

- Law No. 23/96 of 26th July which established oversight in the provision of services of general interest
- Decree-Law No. 90/2009 of 9th April regulating public partnerships between the central state and municipalities
- Decree-Law No. 194/2009 of 20th August referencing the municipal owned services law

- Decree-Law No. 195/2009 of 20th August that revised the state owned services law

## *Independence*

ERSAR is an independent authority with binding powers regarding the regulation of operators and an advisory role to governments regarding national strategy and legislation. Its independence is explicitly stated in statutes, which provides the regulator with the confidence to make decisions free of third party interventions, including being overridden following government assessment. ERSAR is entirely funded through industry fees which are then passed to consumers as a cost, which again provides another level of insulation from unwarranted government interventions. In addition, Board members cannot be removed before the end of their term, except for specific misconduct provided in the statutes (but not on political grounds), while technical staff are employed on the basis of their skill set, not due to political influence or criteria.

ERSAR has the power to issue binding regulations without having to obtain approval from other bodies, including government. ERSAR regulations cover topics such as tariffs and economic regulation, quality of service regulation, drinking water quality, user interface, regulatory compliance, among others. ERSAR regulations do not need approval by other government bodies and their scope of is restricted to operators' actions in terms of service provision. Other overarching new legislation that impacts at the national level needs to be approved by government or through the Parliament. Individual decisions regarding the operators are not subject to approval or official guidance from the government or the Parliament.

Portuguese regulatory policy recognises the natural monopoly elements of the water sector inherent in its network structure. While there is no basic natural monopoly in the waste sector, there are legal monopolies arising from contractual arrangements.

## Mandate and role

### *Regulatory objectives, scope and model*

As described above, the regulator was established as part of a much broader process of regulatory reform aimed at building strong, technically efficient, and universal W and WS sectors. It was intended to protect the public interest in recognition of the fundamental role water and waste services play in society and to make service providers more accountable. With the existence of private operators and major structural change being undertaken an effective, strong, independent regulator was also seen as an important measure to accompany the privatisation measures. Also one of the important roles of the regulator is to provide rationality and harmonise practices and criteria for service provision.

---

**Box 4.2. ERSAR mission**

Public water supply, urban wastewater management and municipal waste management are public services essential to the well-being, public health and, finally, collective security of the population and economic activities, as well as to the protection of the environment.

These services must respect the principles of universal access, uninterrupted and high quality of service and efficient and equitable prices.

ERSAR aims to:

- Ensure the protection of the water and waste sector users, always trying to avoid abuses resulting from the exclusive rights, focusing the control of the quality of the services provided and supervising the tariffs charged to end-users;

- Ensure equal and clear conditions in the access to the water and wastewater services and the operation of these services. This principle also applies to all contracts signed;

- Reinforce the right to general information about the sector and, more precisely, about each operator

*Source*: www.ersar.pt/website_en.

---

The duties and objectives of the regulator are enshrined in legislation (Law No. 10/2014 6th March).

As observed above, there are several types of operators in the W and WS sectors, including:

- Directly managed by municipalities, including municipal services and municipal associations

- Delegated service management with municipal owned corporate companies or companies established in partnership with the State, small scale (parish) run operators and/or user associations

- Concessional arrangements, whereby systems are operated in Public-Private partnerships or through concessions or through other arrangements with private operators.

State and municipal governments share responsibility for WWS within the Portuguese regulatory framework. The State is responsible for the bulk services (multi-municipal systems) while the retail services are responsibility of the municipalities (municipal systems). The three basic management models are referenced above: direct management, delegation and concessions.

This means that ERSAR's remit extends to private owned utilities; state owned utilities, both national and sub-national; all urban water services and rural water services (which include many small scale operators such as local parish and user associations). In undertaking its duties in regard to regulation and ensuring water quality, ERSAR oversees 432 operators in the water and waste sectors and 326 water supply operators in relation to water quality.

The number of operators has reduced considerably in recent years, due to the devolution of delegated management by parishes and users associations (small scale operators) to the municipalities. This reduction also reflects the need to have operators with a more efficient scale, benefitting from economies of scale.

In addition to ensuring quality of services provided through drinking water supply systems, urban wastewater and municipal waste systems by supervising the establishment, management and operation of those systems, ERSAR also is tasked with ensuring the stability and financial sustainability of the various systems.

The regulatory framework ERSAR operates has as objectives:

- The protection of users and consumers through ensuring appropriate quality of service and pricing
- While also undertaking to consider the legitimate business interests of the regulated entities, including their financial viability.

ERSAR's regulatory model aims to focus on structural regulation of the sector, regulation of operators' behaviour and additional regulatory activities around information provision and technical assistance.

*Structural regulation*

ERSAR:

- Monitors national strategies for the sector. It follows the execution of these strategies and reports periodically on their progress and any identified shortcomings.

- Identifies legal aspects that need to be revised and propose its revisions to be approved by the government or Parliament. for example it may prepare or recommend proposals for new legislation, for example, concerning the legal regimes at municipal and multi-municipal levels, technical legislation on the water and waste services and the broader legal regulatory regime (these are done in co-ordination with the Ministry).

*Regulation of the operator's behaviour*

ERSAR:

- Monitors contractual arrangements of operators by assessing how contracts are executed and intervenes, where necessary, in dispute resolution proceedings.

- Undertakes the more traditional economic regulation of operators through price regulation, which aims to achieve efficient and socially acceptable prices while ensuring the operator's' financial and economic sustainability.

- Regulates quality of service, by assessing the service provided to end-users and promoting efficiency by benchmarking operators through the application of a system of indicators.

- Promotes improved water quality through regulation of drinking water, evaluating the quality of water supplied to end-users, the benchmarking of operators and following up on non-compliance.

- ERSAR has sanctioning powers for non-compliance with reporting of information and for non-compliance in timely solving of any drinking water problems.

- Analyses consumers' complaints and promotes conflict resolution between consumers and operators.

*Additional regulatory activities*

ERSAR:

- Gathers and publishes information on the WWS to all operators and ensures that it is accessible to stakeholders and the general public through various channels, including annual reports on the sectors, ERSAR's website, mobile apps.

- Provides technical assistance to operators, regularly engaging in activity and training courses, usually in partnership with universities and research and development centres.
- Promotes innovation and technical research by working with universities and research centres, focused on the priorities of the sector, aimed at improving operators' efficiency and better quality of service.
- Is available to answer questions from all interested stakeholders.

*Economic regulation of W&WS*

This includes:

- regulating tariffs;
- setting quality reference standards for drinking water;
- defining public service obligations (PSOs);
- defining and ensuring technical industry and service standards;
- setting incentive measures in the regulatory framework for the efficient use of water resources and for efficient investment incentives;
- promoting innovative technologies and demand management practices;
- gathering sound data and relevant information;
- monitoring service delivery performance;
- promoting customer engagement and separately undertaking consumer protection and dispute resolution actions;
- supervising contracts;
- ensuring uniform systems of accounts, for example financial accounts to allow availability of comparable and harmonised information regarding costs of service provision;
- analysis of the investment plans and business plans of utilities and carrying out management audits on those utilities.

This is a very broad remit and involves a range of actors, both direct and indirect, requiring a well-established communications framework, information flows and co-ordinated actions.

As would be expected the substantial range of performance information which is collected by the regulator is also made available to the public via its website.

These include:

- Industry and market performance (e.g. network faults);
- Operational and service delivery (e.g. number of inspections);
- Quality of regulatory processes (e.g. compliance with regulation and standards);
- Compliance with legal obligations;
- Economic and financial performance.

ERSAR approves bulk tariffs based on a cost-plus model. New regulatory arrangements will convert the current model for bulk operators into a revenue cap model which incorporates incentives for efficient behaviour. This assessment is subject to public consultation. At retail level, a set of rules has been established regarding the tariff structure and regulated entities must take into account the cost of service and any relevant subsidies, which should be explicitly considered when calculating the tariff. Quality of service is regulated through the tariff system and through sanctions and awards following the approval of the assessment and auditing of the information collected to compute into 16 indicators per service.

## Internal organisation

### *Governance model*

ERSAR is an independent authority established as a Commission model. While the legislation doesn't specify the skillset and experience needed for a member of the board of the authority it establishes that their profile should be based on acknowledged reputation, independence and technical competence, professional experience and appropriate academic background to carry out their functions. In practice directors are expected to bring relevant experience, such as in public sector management, engineering, economics, regulation or the law. There is also a stakeholders' advisory committee, the Advisory Council, where all relevant stakeholders are represented. The council expresses opinions on strategic action plans and on reports of those plans as well as on major regulatory decisions.

The board of directors (Commission members) is supported by a number of operational departments established:

- Vertically by function – (Economical and Financial Analysis Department, Engineering Department – Water Sector, Engineering Department – Waste Sector, Legal Analysis Department and the Water Quality Department);
- Horizontally for support areas – (Strategic Projects Department, Information Technology Department, Administration and Financial and Department and the Secretariat).

As noted there is also an Advisory Council and, as with the majority of economic regulators in the OECD, a statutory auditor. The Advisory Council is currently composed of 35 members, which institutionally represent the major stakeholders in the sector, including public administration, operators, municipalities, professional and technical associations, consumer associations, industrial and agricultural associations, environmental NGOs and recognised experts. The Advisory Council is the consultation mechanism in the definition of the general intervention of the regulator, as well as issuing an opinion about the activities plan, activities report and public accounts, and proposing measures to improve the sector and the activities developed by the regulator.

The term of office for members of the board is set at a non-renewable six years, a doubling of the previous three year renewable limit. The appointment of the agency head and members is made by the government following parliamentary hearings that issue a non-binding decision. Members cannot undertake or hold other employment or appointments outside government and can only be removed subject to a very specific set of grounds incorporated into the statutes via a court procedure or through a government decision following an independent inquiry. These include a general set of issues around malfeasance, mental or physical incapacity, breaches of the act, failure to disclose conflicts and neglect of duties.

There is approximately 75 staff, with 21 employed to undertake mainly administrative tasks while the rest undertake technical work. Staffs are appointed through fair and open competitive processes and the skills set is spread across economics, the law, accounting, engineering, chemistry and social sciences. The agency is now exempt from the usual civil service salary rules following recent changes to the regulator's statutes.

As noted above, ERSAR is entirely funded by the consumers, through the industry, via fees for service and monies from penalties and fines. The fee structure depends on the level of activity of the regulated entity and on the number of customers. While it has separate funding with autonomy in the allocation of its budget, ERSAR is not able to go back to government or entities for additional funding to cover unanticipated shortfalls, such as litigation expenses.

## Accountability mechanisms

ERSAR is accountable to government (for budget measures as it must report annually on its budget to the government), the Parliament and to representatives of the regulated businesses who sit on the Advisory Council. The regulator is required to report at Parliament's request on its performance. In recent years this has occurred at least twice a year. There is a legislative requirement for the regulator to report on its activities yearly and all this information is publically available via ERSAR's web site. It is also required to report on the sector. These documents are then sent to the government, the Parliament, the members of the Advisory Council, operators and other relevant stakeholders. The publications are sent to over 600 institutions yearly.

Legislation requires ERSAR to publish a forward looking action plan, its operational costs and its Governance structure. Decisions of the regulator can be appealed through the courts on the basis of a breach of the law. In addition, there is a process of internal review where operators have a right to reply before the final decisions are made by the Board.

## Inter-institutional co-ordination and collaboration

It becomes obvious from just a cursory examination of the regulatory framework and its numerous actors that ERSAR faces a considerable challenge in engaging with the broad range of stakeholders who have an interest in regulatory outcomes in the regulated sectors. With over 400 regulated entities alone, including a number of municipal and/or quasi-government entities, the regulator is faced with an enormous endeavour. Collaboration and co-ordination with the vast range of interested stakeholders becomes a major task and an important strategic tool for ERSAR.

In the waste sector, ERSAR has established a framework within which it is able work with its main stakeholders via an information management system to collect and treat data. This framework not only promotes greater effectiveness regarding regulation, but also:

- improved stakeholder awareness;
- the achieving and maintaining of synergies;
- greater transparency of procedures;

- the additional collection of information; and
- greater legitimisation of regulation.

## Co-ordination with other arms of government

There are several other government departments that are involved in W&WS. These include:

- Ministry for the Environment and Energy (MAOTE), which is in some management models responsible for providing the service, through the Águas de Portugal holding company but also provides the broader policy and sector wide strategic planning; it works with the regulator in developing new sector wide legislation
- Municipalities, which provide retail services in some cases and also agree to concessions to other operators.
- The Portuguese Environmental Agency (APA), which exercises its mandate in relation to water planning, water abstraction and discharge licensing and shares responsibility with ERSAR in regards to monitoring of environmental sustainability of the regulated services
- The Competition Authority, which enforces competition laws in the WWS and works with ERSAR in assessing mergers, expansion into other non-regulated markets, and in procurement procedures for water management services.
- The health authorities, who are responsible for public health regarding possible events of impact of poor drinking water quality.

In order to ensure effective co-ordination between the regulator and the ministry, the regulator is actively involved in formulating policy and in any subsequent refinement of that policy because of the vast amount of information and knowledge the regulator has about the services. ERSAR also provides advice to the Ministry and the minister on sector issues. It is also open to the ministry to call for co-ordination meetings with the regulator when this is deemed necessary.

Regulatory decisions are recognised under the statutes as having been made independently of government, with no intervention allowed by through use of political power. The support role ERSAR undertakes for the ministry is related to technical advice in terms of service provision, without any policy decision intervention.

The enabling legislation allows the regulator to authorise subcontracted staff to undertake specific functions, such as inspections or compliance operations, mandated by the regulator. These are limited however to the field tasks of collection of information to fundament subsequent regulatory decisions. It also allows ERSAR to enter into agreements with other bodies and to share information with other regulators where it is deemed relevant and appropriate.

To ensure effective co-ordination and clarity, there are also other mechanisms in place such as agreements that detail the respective roles and co-operation arrangements with other jurisdictional regulators (for example, with the Competition authority). There are also regular meetings of the Advisory Council and the usual ad hoc meetings on specific issues as they arise.

As mentioned above the ERSAR Advisory Council includes representatives of all levels of government. The Advisory Council is involved in discussing and assessing the strategy and activities of the regulator and provides an additional institutional measure to underpin communication with other government actors.

### *Strategies for co-ordination and collaboration*

Co-ordination across the range of stakeholders is essential in achieving the broader policy goals of the government in regard to the W&WS sectors. In addition to the numerous municipalities and the regulated entities, there are several other government departments that are involved in the WWS. Given the crossover of interests and the ubiquitous nature of water and wastewater in society and the economy, a well-developed co-ordination and communication strategy is essential.

ERSAR has a well-thought through strategic collaboration framework that requires it to take account of following:

- Government and parliament, holders of political power and those responsible for public policy definition and the approval of legislation;

- Public administration, particularly in terms of clarifying its competencies to lead and co-ordinate the policy of water and waste services, as well as the articulation of activities in the boundary areas of their respective mandates;

- The relationship with the utilities which are subject to regulation and that should be based on the principles of co-operation, mutual respect and transparency, with resulting benefits to users and society more generally;

- The users and users associations, the recipients of these essential public services, particularly through the participation and clarification of doubts and resolution of potential complaints;
- Associations representing economic activities, which are also recipients of these essential public services;
- Non-governmental environmental protection organisations, with regard to the potential environmental impacts of these services;
- The most relevant technical and scientific institutions and associations in the sectors, potential partners for capacity building and innovation, particularly in terms of co-operation, collaboration and association, within the scope of their duties, as embodied in studies, training, audits and joint publications;
- Peer national and international regulatory bodies, when this is shown to be necessary or useful in carrying out its respective duties, particularly the exchange of regulatory experiences.

By involving these entities through sharing of knowledge, efforts aimed at coordinating activities and efforts and agreeing to the complementary nature of some responsibilities, the regulator greatly enhances its own work.

The provision of water and waste services, besides involving the intervention of the regulator is also subject to the intervention of different public bodies. This involves activities with an impact in areas which are the responsibility of environmental, water resources, waste management, and public health authorities (supply of drinking water), consumer protection (provision of essential public services) and competition (public markets).

The correct functioning of the sectors therefore has to include a clear understanding between the different public bodies involved, underpinned by definition of their respective roles and responsibilities, so as to avoid any overlaps or omissions. It should also enable cross-organisational synergies to be captured and the reconciliation of the various goals of each public agency or Department, taking into account the provision of water and waste services for society at least cost possible.

Due to its importance in ensuring a suitable institutional framework, with a clear assignment of responsibilities for the all of the public entities involved, the steps taken to ensure a seamless relationship and clarity of roles between ERSAR and the environmental, water resources, waste management, public health, consumer protection and competition authorities are central to ERSAR's collaborative arrangements.

ERSAR has been developing practices to bring these approaches to life. Some are based on legislated requirements while others have been instituted informally building on relationships with other players. For example, in the waste water sector ERSAR is statutorily required to collaborate with APA in defining the values used by the selective collection company responsible for recyclables management (*Sociedade Ponto Verde*) to provide for compensation to collection operators for the extra cost of collecting recyclables in their waste.

In regard to sharing of information the basis of analysis is different in each authority (ERSAR deals with operators while APA analyses at the basin level). This leads to the continuing existence of barriers to the complete sharing of information through interconnected databases. Currently sharing of information occurs ad hoc, with each party providing information requested by the other. ERSAR has, however, now developed as is continuing to develop systems that allow for the provision of access to partner institutions to the broad suite of information available to ERSAR.

A set of principles sets the framework for ERSAR's operational relationships with its main collaborators. These include:

- Co-ordination in regards to, and where appropriate joint development of, legislation and regulation for the water services with the other authorities' legislation and regulations;

- Co-ordination in the implementation of public policies for water services with public policies that intersect;

- Co-ordination and collaboration in the collection, validation, processing and dissemination of water services information with relevant information collected by the other authority;

- Clearly articulated boundaries in regards to the management of water sources aimed at the production of drinking water and all associated information, for example, geographical location, protection of sources, monitoring and licensing of use;

- Clearly articulated boundaries in regards to responsibility for overseeing the abstraction of surface, underground and even coastal water resources, for the purposes of supplying water for human consumption;

- Clearly articulated boundaries in regards to responsibility for managing discharges of waste water into surface, underground and coastal water resources, or into the soil;

- Reporting by the other authorities concerning inspection activities carried out on water service utilities, which are important for the regulator's activity, and, vice versa, namely by reporting situations which may indicate the presence of infringements. This includes consumer protection and competition authorities sharing of information that may point to breeches in the others statutes;

- In the consumer protection sphere there is a requirement for joint promotion of institutionalised arbitration of consumer disputes.

### *Co-ordination and collaboration with the APA*

The environmental authority (APA) has the main responsibility for proposing, developing and monitoring the integrated management of environmental policies and sustainable development. It must do so in a manner that takes into account other sectoral policies while also recognising the potential competing interests of other public and private entities. It must take into account the protection and recovery of the environment and the provision of high quality services to Portuguese citizens.

In Portugal the APA also has responsibilities as the water resources authority so that the ERSAR/APA relationship is a core one and a good example of co-ordination and collaboration between authorities.

While the focus of the relationship between the two bodies is on both the use of water resources as raw material for the production of drinking water, as well as the use of water resources as a receiving body for wastewater, it needs to be viewed in the context of the broader environmental policy.

Good institutional co-ordination and interaction requires a clear delineation in the areas of responsibility of those bodies as well as clear direction and joint engagement in developing structured instruments, implementing public policies, interpreting legislation, regulations and contracts and also with regard to information management.

In regard to the need for clear identification of the agencies' operational boundaries, the interventions APA undertakes as the water resources authority are focused on the set of measures noted in the preceding paragraph. These form the basic interface with water services, as they do with other water users, such as agriculture, industry, energy production, transportation, tourism and leisure.

On the other hand, ERSAR's interventions are distinct, focusing on the regulation of water supply and wastewater services, involving suppliers and users, and concerning itself with the sustainability of those services from an integrated perspective and within a context of effectiveness and efficiency. In effect it is regulating just one of the various water sectors. The boundaries that set the framework for the different interventions have been made legally clear and embodied mainly through two intersecting points; water abstraction and the discharge of wastewater, activities that are subject to licensing by the respective authorities.

As for co-ordinated development in the structuring of various instruments, such as the setting up of policies, approval of legislation or even the definition of specific procedures, these should ideally be subject to joint analysis by the appropriate bodies before their approval. This enables the achievement of optimal outcomes through the bringing together of the different perspectives and should aid in preventing unanticipated outcomes and providing a balance between potentially competing viewpoints. For example, the drawing up or revision of water resources legislation requires not only suitable assessment of its environmental effectiveness but also an economic impact assessment of the water services sectors, the stakeholders involved and finally the users, through cost-benefit studies.

The two authorities are represented in the strategic plans for the sector. At the operational level, there are several specific meetings between both authorities to discuss topics and issues common to both. All the legislation impacting on the water and waste water sectors is also subject to consultation with both authorities.

The two authorities undertake prior consultation whenever the drawing up of policies, the approval of legislation or even specific procedures in areas of direct interaction between water resources and water services is concerned. The authorities' statutes provide for both to be involved in technical support for the legislative process and this occurs in practice.

Various bodies involved in interpreting legislation, regulations and contracts, should not, for obvious reasons, have different interpretations when considering the same or related matters. The risk of lack of uniformity is one of the reasons that it is important to set clear boundaries and where the resources authority is involved these are going to be primarily associated with issues involving abstraction and discharge of water resources. This issue relates not just to interpretation of legislation but in the application legislative instruments by the two authorities. Examples include the use of water resources by entities providing water services, licences for private abstractions in the case of public water services availability, the desalination of sea water, wastewater discharges and the production and use of treated wastewater.

In regard to information management, there is, on the one hand, the need to avoid overlapping information requests to the utilities by different entities and, on the other hand, the need to ensure mutual access to information systems. Good public administration practices again consider that the collection of the same information or similar information, at different times using different procedures should not be undertaken by different bodies where this can be avoided. Unnecessary compliance costs may be imposed through failure to recognise the need to ensure co-ordinated actions in the management of information.

This overlapping information request issue arises regularly in regard to other bodies within the sectors, such as the consumer protection and competition authorities. ERSAR's leadership commit to strong relationships that encourage sharing of information and commitment on the part of authority staff to consider the burden of its information requests and to consider whether this information can be obtained through other public administration bodies.

For example, it is the duty of the water resources authority to carry out an inventory and maintain a record of the public water domain and set up and keep up-to-date information and water resource management systems, as well as promote communication and ensure the dissemination of information to ensure knowledge of water resources in terms of catchment areas. The regulator has the duty to co-ordinate and carry out the collection and dissemination of information regarding public water supply and wastewater sectors and their respective utilities. Co-ordination is therefore important in the sharing of information for the purposes of the authorities.

APA in its water resources management role is generally responsible for the development and application of national policies in the area of water resources and the general co-ordination, planning and licensing in the management of water resources, with a view to ensuring in particular its protection and proper resource planning. As such, it aims to preserve water resources and ensure their rational use.

### *Co-ordination and collaboration with the public health authority*

The public health authority normally has responsibility for the general co-ordination and planning of activities promoting health, preventing disease, and providing health care. Its duties may involve legislation, guidance, co-ordination and monitoring. It should intervene in the protection of public health, in the prevention of diseases and in health promotion. In addition it should aim to identify and control risk factors in situations which may cause or increase serious harm to the health of the citizens or that of particular population clusters, as may be the case with the water and waste services.

## *Co-ordination and collaboration with the consumer protection authority*

The consumer protection authority normally has the responsibility of contributing towards the development and enforcement of national consumer protection policy and law. It aims to ensure a high level of protection for all consumers, particularly through monitoring the activity of consumer associations; arbitration centres for consumer conflicts; other extrajudicial resolution mechanisms for these conflicts; and consumer information centres.

It should be noted while the responsibility of this authority in the promotion of consumer protection takes place within the framework of services in general, particularly essential public services, the economic regulation and quality of service under the responsibility of the regulator seeks to safeguard the rights and interests of all users of water and waste services. This corresponds to a wider group than that of just consumers, including all users, particularly commercial and industrial bodies.

ERSARS's activities are also carried out within a more integrated framework, bringing an economic and environmental sustainability perspective to the assessment of the services.

## *Co-ordination and collaboration with the competition authority*

The water and waste services regulator should be subject to a principle of subsidiarity with regard to the competition authority. Its function is also to promote and defend competition, to respond to gaps in the market, besides ensuring the carrying out of public interest goals not necessarily ensured by the market, starting with ensuring the on-going and unbroken supply of certain goods and services essential to the community.

One of ERSAR's tasks is to promote competition and contribute to the establishment of well-functioning markets where natural or legal monopolies are the norm to help develop and support the progressive opening of these sectors and the development of healthy competition where that is possible. It should be noted that the progressive adoption of competition in the regulated sectors will ultimately reduce ERSAR's role in regards to the competition authority. Conceptually, sectoral regulation will have reached its final goal when it is no longer necessary for society.

However, while this is theoretically possible within a long-term perspective, in practical terms this is unlikely to eventuate.

The fact that the public water and waste services operate within a natural or legal monopoly market structure and under the scope of exclusivity of rights does not exclude the need to consider measures to introduce competition.

The management of these services may allow for the existence of competition and access to the market, particularly when the service holders (State, municipalities, etc.) decide to involve private utilities to manage systems through a delegation or a concession contract, to participate in the capital of companies integrated in the State owned business sector or the simple provision of services, typically infrastructure operation through a services provision contract.

In any of the described situations, competition should be ensured and maximised through public procurement rules, and it assumes special importance for issues such as:

- Non-discrimination, transparency and equal treatment within the scope of public procurement procedures, which seek to enable the participation of the greatest number of competitors in conditions involving equality of opportunities.

- Time limits or termination clauses in contractual arrangements. Limitations on time need to seek a balance between investor certainty in terms of the return on and recovery of investment, which is in turn a driving factor in terms of the attractiveness of the contract for private bodies, and market development's that allow an increase in the instances of competition within the market.

- The existence of limits on the alteration of contracts, so as to prevent the distortion of the rules and underlying principles which led to the choice of the winning bidder. This is again an important factor in underpinning investor confidence and providing a degree of certainty to the market.

In some ancillary water and waste systems service provision markets (subcontracting), competition problems may arise through the existence of significant buyer power on the part of the contracting entities. This is often a concern in markets that display attributes of oligopsony. This may lead to restrictions in competitive tensions in these markets, for example those involving construction, the supply of products and equipment and public infrastructure consultants.

Portuguese policy recognises that utilities authorised by law to manage services of general economic interest or which have the form of a legal monopoly should remain subject to competition rules, in so far as this does not constitute an obstacle to their compliance, in law or in fact, with the particular mission which has been entrusted to them. This issue is particularly important with regard to the application of the State aid system.

Finally, unbundling of activities similar to that which was undertaken in the electricity and rail transportation sectors may be usefully considered in order to reduce the scope of the monopoly and liberalise certain activities.

The competition authority is normally responsible for the regulation of market competition, including the public drinking supply of water, waste water management, and solid waste management services and the various associated markets. The application of competition rules should be ensured, with regard to principle of the market economy and that of free competition, taking into account the efficient functioning of the markets, a high level of technical progress and the achievement of the greatest benefit to the users.

*Ministerial relationships*

Relations with the Minister are based on the independence of the regulator. ERSAR meets periodically with the Minister to discuss relevant topics about the sector and pending issues. These meetings may occur both at the request of the Minister or at the request of ERSAR and are mostly related to strategic collaboration aspects or inter-ministerial issues, since ERSAR does not usually interact with other ministers.

## Concluding insights

The complexity of modern public administration, coming in part as it does from the rise in the interrelatedness of various policy measures that flow from different public entities, requires a substantial investment on the part of regulators in co-operative measures and actions involving those entities. These may include other enforcement bodies and regulators, Departments of State and Ministers. As this case study demonstrates close co-operation requires institutional arrangements that support co-ordinated and collaborative approaches to common challenges. It also shows the need to set down clear boundaries in regard to responsibilities in developing and enforcing policies.

Communication is essential in providing certainty to market participants and helping to prevent unintended consequences from failure to recognise the potential impact of actions taken by one body on the operations of another and the follow through implications for the markets involved.

The role of the leadership and senior management of the agency is an essential element of a successful program of co-ordination and collaboration. Professor Malcolm Sparrow in *The Regulatory Craft* identifies a number of issues relating to collaborative arrangements between agencies. Agencies and authorities must be willing to move outside their traditional silos and be willing to share the limelight with others (Sparrow, 2000). This is an aspect rarely mentioned but an important underlying aspect of the leadership of an authority in building trust with others who operate in the sector.

# Bibliography

OECD (2015), *The Governance of Water Regulators*, OECD Studies on Water, OECD Publishing, Paris, http://dx.doi.org/10.1787/9789264231092-en

Sparrow, M. (2000), *The regulatory craft: controlling risks, solving problems and managing compliance*, Brookings Institution Press, Washington.

# Chapitre 5

## The UK Office of Rail and Road (ORR)

> *This chapter presents some of the arrangements and practices related to accountability and transparency put in place by the UK Office of Rail and Road.*

## Regulatory framework, objectives and functions

The ORR is the economic, safety and health regulator for the rail industry in Great Britain.[1] It is an independent body with a range of functions stated in various Acts,[2] along with the associated duties that govern the public interest aspects in how it exercises those functions. In addition to the more traditional role as an economic regulator of monopoly infrastructure, the ORR is also the national safety regulator for the industry and is the consumer and competition authority, working with the Competition and Markets Authority (CMA) in its application of the Competition Act 1998 which extends to services relating to railways.

From 1 April 2015 the ORR took on new responsibilities for overseeing the performance of Highways England. This is the government-owned company that runs the highways network in England (Wales, Scotland and Northern Ireland have separate arrangements). ORR's operating name changed from the Rail Regulation to the Office of Rail of regulating rail as described below to reflect its new roads function, which is founded in the Infrastructure Act 2015.

The ORR also operates under European Union (EU) law and works to influence this law to achieve the best framework response for the United Kingdom and to implement EU law within the United Kingdom. The EU aims to create a single market within Europe that is both efficient and competitive. To this end it focuses on actions to:

- Open rail markets;
- Promote competition;
- Confront barriers to entry;
- Harmonise technical (interoperability) standards;
- Harmonise safety standards and associated certification.

The main statutory duties that the ORR must take into account when undertaking its functions are listed in Section 4 of the Railways Act 1993 (RA93) for its economic regulatory activities and for safety in the Railways Act 2005 (the 2005 Act) and the Health and Safety at Work etc Act 1974 (www.hse.gov.uk/legislation/hswa.htm). Duties are regarded as entailing public interest considerations and may be thought of in some respects as the objectives of the legislative framework, while functions refer to the tasks and activities undertaken.

The ORR's independence is provided for in its enabling legislation, guaranteeing it is protected from direct political interference in its decision making.

The 2005 Act amended RA93, changing the statutory framework for the periodic review of access charges and transferring the rail specific health and safety regulation to the ORR. Those amendments also transferred responsibility for monitoring and enforcing license conditions in respect to consumer protection. The ORR also has a legislated mandate to provide advice and assistance to the Secretary of State for Transport, Scottish Ministers and the National Assembly of Wales.

The ORR summarises its vision as ensuring Britain's railways deliver "safety, performance and efficiency equivalent to the best comparable railways in the world". It sets out six strategic objectives that focus on safety, improving the experience of passengers and value for money achieved by all those using the railway and strategic road network, and supporting sustainable growth and investment. The ORR follows existing principles of better regulation, to make regulation risk and evidence-based, to support industry in meeting its obligations but take appropriate enforcement action when necessary.

The following sections outline the legislative framework in which the ORR operates. In considering the ORR's functions and duties the following points should be taken into account.

- The duties are different when the ORR is exercising its economic and its safety functions, although one of the economic duties relates to "the need to protect all persons from dangers arising from the operation of railways". There is currently no equivalent economic duty to be considered in the exercise of safety functions.

- The application of the economic duties to the ORR's competition and consumer functions is not straightforward and further details are not included for the purposes of this case study. As with other public bodies in the UK, the ORR is also subject to duties under the equalities legislation.

- Nomenclature – the numerous legislation that set out the ORR's duties and functions use various different words to describe them, including purposes and objectives. Some of its functions are also described as "duties" in a public law sense. For ease of reference, this case study uses the terms that are generally used within the ORR –"duties" means public interest considerations and "functions" means what the ORR does.

## Objectives and duties[3]

### Major legislation

**RA93** – this Act contains most of ORR's functions including, but not limited to:

- Licensing;
- access agreements;
- review of access charges; and
- enforcement.

*Section 4 of RA93* also contains the statutory duties which the ORR must take into account in exercising its economic regulatory functions.

**Railways Act 2005 (RA05)** – this Act largely amends the **RA93**. The Act made a number of changes to the ORR's regulatory framework, including:

- a change to the statutory framework for periodic reviews of access charges;
- transferring responsibility for rail-specific health and safety regulation from the Health and Safety Executive to the ORR;
- creation of additional functions for the ORR, including a role in dealing with proposals for the closure of passenger services, passenger networks and stationsstation, track or level crossing closures;
- transferring responsibility for monitoring and enforcing the licence conditions concerning consumer protection from the Strategic Rail Authority; and
- providing advice and assistance to the Secretary of State for Transport, Scottish Ministers and the National Assembly of Wales.

**Health and Safety at Work Act 1974 (HSWA 1974)** – this is the primary piece of health and safety legislation in Great Britain. The Act sets out the general duties which employers have towards employees and members of the public, and employees have to themselves and to each other. These duties are qualified in the Act by the principle of 'so far as is reasonably practicable'. In other words, an employer does not have to take measures to avoid or reduce the risk if they are technically impossible or if the time, trouble or cost of the measures would be grossly disproportionate to the risk. Health and safety regulations made under this Act contain more detailed provisions. The Act provides the framework for the regulation of industrial health and safety in the UK which is relevant to the ORR as the health and safety regulator for the rail industry.

**Railways and other Guided Transport Systems (Safety) Regulations 2006 (ROGS)** – provide the regulatory regime for rail safety, including the mainline railway, metros (including London Underground), tramways, light rail and heritage railways. The regulations implement the European Railway Safety Directive (2004/49/EC), which aims to establish a common approach to rail safety and support the development of a single market for rail transport services in Europe. The regulations require most railway operators (known as transport operators) to maintain a safety management system (SMS) and hold a safety certificate or authorisation indicating the SMS has been accepted by the ORR.

**Rail Vehicle Accessibility (Non-Interoperable Rail System) Regulations 2010 (RVAR 2010)** – set out the accessibility standards to which new non-mainline (and older rail vehicles as and when they are refurbished) must comply. The ORR enforces these Regulations and the requirements in the Persons of Reduced Mobility Technical Specification for Interoperability (PRM TSI) which cover heavy rail.

As noted in the introduction, the ORR is also the national safety authority for Britain's railways under EU law.

*ORR's economic duties*

The ORR's main statutory economic duties, derived from the preceding legislation including RA 93, cover a wide range of issues which together make up "the public interest" for the purposes of exercising its economic functions. A number of general points to note:

- The duties only apply when ORR is exercising its functions. They do not require ORR to take action in the absence of any function. However, there are some very general functions, for example keeping the provision of railway services in Great Britain and elsewhere under review.

- The only overriding duty of the ORR relates to the channel tunnel rail link (now generally referred to as High Speed One (HS1)) and exercising its functions so as not to impede the "performance of any development agreement". To date, this has only rarely arisen and it does not apply to the exercise of its functions for HS1. Subject to this overriding duty, there is no hierarchy between the ORR's other duties even though there are certain differences in the statutory language. Given the range of duties, on occasions they may conflict. The ORR is required to determine on a case by case basis which duties are relevant and what weight to give to each of them. This means that decision makers may consider different duties to be relevant or to have greater or lesser weight in relation to decisions about different matters – or to decisions about similar matters taken at different times or in different circumstances.

- The ORR could decide to adopt a policy to give particular weight to particular duties in particular circumstances (for example, the interests of users or promoting efficiency and economy on the part of entities providing railway services). That would be lawful provided the decision was supported by rational reasons for doing so and that ORR continued to consider in each case whether the circumstances required departure from the policy.

*Duties under section 4 of the RA93*

The ORR shall have a duty to exercise the functions assigned or transferred to it under the RA93 or by virtue of this Part or the Railways Act 2005 that are not safety functions in the manner which it considers best calculated –

- To promote improvements in railway service performance;

- Otherwise to protect the interests of users of railway services;

- To promote the use of the railway network in Great Britain for the carriage of passengers and goods, and the development of that railway network, to the greatest extent which it considers economically practicable;

- To contribute to the development of an integrated system of transport of passengers and goods;

- To contribute to the achievement of sustainable development;

- To promote efficiency and economy on the part of entities providing railway services;

- To promote competition in the provision of railway services for the benefit of users of railway services;

- To promote measures designed to facilitate the making by passengers of journeys which involve use of the services of more than one passenger service operator;

- To impose on the operators of railway services the minimum restrictions which are consistent with the performance of ORR's functions under Part 1 RA93 and RA05; and
- To enable entities providing railway services to plan the future of their businesses with a reasonable degree of assurance.

Without prejudice to the general duties above, the ORR should exercise its economic functions:

- To take into account the need to protect all persons from dangers arising from the operation of railways;
- To protect the interests of users and potential users of services for the carriage of passengers by railway provided by a private sector operator, otherwise than under a franchise agreement, in respect of the prices charged for travel by means of those services, and the quality of the service provided.

The ORR shall be under a duty in exercising the functions assigned or transferred to it under or by virtue of this Part of the RA93 or the RA05 that are not safety functions:

- To have regard to the effect on the environment of activities connected with the provision of railway services;
- To protect the interests of entities providing services for the carriage of passengers or goods by railway in their use of any railway facilities which are for the time being vested in a private sector operator, in respect of the prices charged for such use and the quality of the service provided;

The Office of Rail Regulation shall also be under a duty in exercising the functions assigned or transferred to it under this Part or the RA05 that are not safety functions:

- In the case of functions other than its safety functions as an enforcing authority for the purposes of the HSWA 1974, to have regard to any general guidance given to it by the Secretary of State about railway services or other matters relating to railways;
- To act in a manner which it considers will not render it unduly difficult for persons who are holders of network licences to finance any activities or proposed activities of theirs in relation to which ORR has functions;

- To have regard to any notified strategies and policies of the National Assembly of Wales and the ability of the National Assembly of Wales to carry out its functions;

- To have regard to any general guidance given by the Secretary of State, or Scottish Ministers in relation to Scottish railway services, about railway services or other matters relating to railways;

- To have regard to the funds available to the Secretary of State for the purposes of his functions in relation to railways or railways services;

- To have regard to the ability of the Mayor of London and Transport for London to carry out the functions conferred or imposed on them by or under any enactment;

- To have regard, in particular, to the interests of persons who are disabled in relation to services for the carriage of passengers by railway or to station services; and

- To have regard to the interests, in securing value for money, of the users or potential users of railway services, of persons providing railway services, of the persons who make available the resources and funds and of the general public.

It is self-evident from this wide range of duties that the ORR has a significant stakeholder base that, it could be assumed, have different requirements in terms of mechanisms to demonstrate accountability and different levels of expectation as to the level of engagement. This is a major challenge for all modern regulators but especially so for one like the ORR with such a diverse set of responsibilities.

*Other duties*

**Section 21 of the Channel Tunnel Rail Link Act 1996** provides that ORR shall have an overriding duty to exercise its regulatory functions in such a manner as not to impede the performance of any development agreement.

**Section 22 of the Crossrail Act 2008** provides that section 4(1) of RA93 shall be treated as including the objective of facilitating the construction of Crossrail. It also provides that ORR shall consult the Secretary of State about this aspect of the duty.

**Section 72 of the Regulatory Enforcement and Sanctions Act 2008** requires ORR to keep its functions under review and secure that in exercising these functions that ORR does not:

- impose unnecessary burdens; or
- maintain burdens considered to have become unnecessary.

ORR also has a new equalities duty under **Section 149 of the Equality Act 2010** which requires it to have due regard to the need to:

- eliminate discrimination, harassment, victimisation and any other conduct that is prohibited by or under this Act
- advance equality of opportunity between persons who share a relevant protected characteristic and persons who do not share it (relevant protected characteristics are – age; disability; gender reassignment; pregnancy and maternity; race; religion or belief; sex; sexual orientation) and
- foster good relations between persons who share a relevant protected characteristic and persons who do not share it

## *ORR's safety duties*

It is ORR's responsibility to ensure that those responsible to make Britain's railways safe for passengers and to provide a safe place for staff to work comply with the law. ORR regulates health and safety for the entire mainline rail network in Britain, as well as London Underground, light rail, trams and the heritage sector.

Section 1 of Health and Safety at Work Act 1974 sets out general health and safety objectives. These are more focussed than ORR's economic duties and include "securing the health, safety and welfare of persons at work" and "protecting [others] against risks to health or safety arising out of or in connection with the activities of persons at work". These objectives are called HSWA's general purposes.

The railway safety purposes, established by the RA05, are so much of HSWA's general purposes as relate to the risks relevant to or connected with:

- securing the proper construction and safe operation of railways, tramways etc;
- securing the proper construction and safe operation of locomotives, rolling stock or other vehicles used, or to be used, on such systems;
- protecting the public (whether or not they are passengers) from personal injury and other risks arising from the construction and operation of such systems;

- protecting persons at work from personal injury and other risks so arising.

It is worth noting that the RA05 specifies the "railway safety purposes" at a very detailed level by contrast with the very general HSWA purposes. It is intended that the railway safety purposes are effectively carved out of the general purposes so that ORR's safety remit does not overlap with that of the Health and Safety Executive (HSE).

The RA05 sets out ORR's principal safety functions in very general terms. These include to do such things and make such arrangements as it considers appropriate for the railway safety purposes and to assist and encourage persons concerned with matters relevant to any of those purposes to further them. It is also worth noting that one of ORR's principal safety functions includes submitting such proposals as it considers appropriate for the making of regulations for the railway safety purposes to the appropriate authority, usually to the Department for Transport.

## *Functions and powers*

### *ORR's economic functions*

#### Network Rail regulation[4]

ORR holds Network Rail to account for delivering what it promised – at the amount it agreed to do it for under the 5 year periodic review set by ORR – and requires it to provide passengers with a punctual, reliable service. ORR does this by

- holding Network Rail to account for the management of the network by enforcing licence conditions including, where necessary, imposing penalties

- As a competition authority for rail, ORR has enforcement powers derived from Competition Act 1998, the Enterprise Act 2002 and under Articles 101 and 102 of the Treaty on the Functioning of the European Union

- modifying Network Rail's network licence

- issuing approvals and consents under licence conditions/terms

- conducting a periodic review of the charges it can impose on train operating companies for accessing the network: that is setting the contractual and financial framework within which Network Rail operates the network by establishing, the funding it required for a five-year period and the incentives needed to encourage Network Rail to efficiently deliver and outperform its expected activities

## Track Access[5]

The ORR ensures passenger and freight train operating companies have fair and non-discriminate access to the rail network and that best use is made of capacity.

If a railway operator wants to access the railway network, it must agree an access contract with Network Rail which is approved by ORR. Alternatively, if the parties cannot agree access terms, the train company may ask ORR for a direction. Under Sections 17 to 22A of the RA93, ORR:

- Approves and/ or directs new track access contracts and amendments to existing contracts

- Determines appeals under The Railways Infrastructure (Access and Management) Regulations 2005. These Regulations open up access at previously exempt facilities under The RA93 as amended, such as those at ports and terminals and other freight depots and networks. The Regulations allow for, amongst other things, a right of appeal to ORR for any applicant that thinks it has been wrongly denied access to a facility or service or that the terms for obtaining access are unreasonable or discriminatory. Appeals can also be brought against an infrastructure manager's charging system, or charging matters associated with access to unregulated facilities or services.

- Regulates access charges under Access and Management Regulations

- Ensures that the Network Code provides appropriate contractual certainty for all affected parties and does not benefit one contractual party to a greater extent than another

- Determines appeals under the Network Code

## Depot and Station Access[6]

In exercising its functions under sections 17 to 22A of the RA93, the ORR regulates access to station and light maintenance depots by approving station and depot access agreements:

- Approve and or direct new depot and station access contracts and amendments to existing contracts where covered by the Railways Act

- Determine appeals under The Railway Infrastructure (Access and Management) Regulations 2005

## Licensing[7]

Section 6 of the Railways Act 1993 makes it an offense to act as the operator of a railway asset, other than a passenger train or freight train within the scope of the Railway (Licensing of Railway Undertakings) Regulations 2005 (the Regulations), without holding a licence or a licence exemption granted under the Act.

ORR's statutory licensing functions include:

- Granting licences and licence exemptions under the Railways Act and European licences and Statement of National Regulatory Provisions (SNRPs) under 2005 Regulations

- Modifying licences

- Enforcing licence conditions – ORR has substantial powers at its disposal to enforce railway and safety legislation. ORR's economic enforcement powers are outlined in the RA93 under the following sections:

    - **Section 55** sets out what it may do if it chooses to use its licence enforcement powers, particularly for orders issued by ORR for securing compliance

    - **Section 56** sets out procedural requirements for section 55 orders

    - **Section 57** outlines the validity and effect of section 55 orders

    - **Section 58** sets out ORR's power to require information for purposes of section 55 and 57(A) penalties

- Issuing approvals and consents under licence terms/conditions

As a competition authority for rail, ORR has enforcement powers derived from the Competition Act 1998, the Enterprise Act 2002 and under Articles 101 and 102 of the Treaty on the Functioning of the European Union. Section 68 of the RA93 places a duty on ORR to investigate any alleged or apprehended contravention of a licence condition.

HS1 Regulation

ORR:

- approves all new framework agreements and revisions to existing framework agreements (track access contracts covering the reservation of capacity for more than one timetable period of six months). These are the documents which allow access to HS1 network

- also has an appeal role in respect of the terms of track access and more generally under The Railways Infrastructure (Access and Management) Regulations 2005

- regulates HS1 Limited through its Concession Agreement including:
  - access regulation
  - access charges reviews
  - network regulation/asset management
  - monitoring and reporting

Competition and Consumer issues[8]

ORR:

- works to ensure that the rail market is competitive and fair – for passengers, freight customers, railway operators and taxpayers.

- It has powers under both consumer and competition law with regard to the railways. The ORR has extensive powers to investigate companies believed to be involved in anti-competitive activities. Complaints are investigated under the Competition Act 1998.

- Consumer law aims to ensure that businesses are fair and open in their dealings with consumers. ORR powers cover rail passengers and the companies they deal with. ORR is a designated enforcer under Part 8 of the Enterprise Act 2002. Its powers enable it to stop breaches of a range of consumer protection laws where there is evidence of passengers as a group being put at an unfair disadvantage. Key consumer laws include the Consumer Rights Act 2015 and the Consumer Protection from Unfair Trading Regulations 2008. The latter regulations prohibit some practices outright, such as misleading advertising and contain a general ban on "practices which contravene the requirements of professional diligence".

Investments[9]

The ORR has a role in making sure the investment infrastructures are in place, and once agreed, projects are delivered on time and budget. The ORR therefore has:

- powers to issue directions requiring person to provide a new facility or to improve or develop existing facility (powers never yet used);

- mechanisms under section 16a of the RA93 which allows it to direct the improvement or construction of a railway facility; and

- approvals criteria that set out the conditions that must be met when an approval from the ORR is necessary. The ORR also publishes how it monitors the use of the investment framework and projects promoted using it.

Closures of passenger services, passenger networks and stations

The ORR:

- ensures that the consultation undertaken in accordance with the closures guidance, has been carried out appropriately;

- evaluates the assessment made to ensure that the published methodology has been followed correctly; and

- considers whether the proposed closure represents poor or low value for money in comparison with retention

Other European law

The ORR ensures fair and equal access to the rail network and services, monitoring competition in rail services (including freight) and dealing with appeals on access and charges.

The Channel Tunnel Intergovernmental Commission (IGC)

The ORR provides the IGC's secretariat and several of its members. The ORR also provides all but one of the UK members of the Channel Tunnel Safety Authority (CTSA, which is IGC's statutory independent safety advisory body) and all the UK members of IGC's joint economic committee (which advises IGC on access regulation).

The British and French governments announced in 2014 that the ORR will take new responsibilities for regulating the UK half of the Channel Tunnel later; at the same time the *Autorité de Régulation des Activités*

*Ferroviaires* (ARAF – the french rail regulator) will become responsible for the French part of the link. This arrangement takes effect in 2016.

### Advise and assist

The ORR has an obligation to provide information, advice and assistance to the Secretary of State for Transport as well as the Welsh and Scottish governments on railways, railway services and railway safety.

### Keeping markets under review[10]

The ORR has a range of functions and responsibilities to keep railway markets under review and to take appropriate measures where markets are not working to the benefit of users or funders.

## *ORR's safety functions*

### Principal railway safety functions

ORR:

- to do such things and make such arrangements as ORR considers appropriate for the railway safety purposes; and
- To assist and encourage persons concerned with matters relevant to any of those purposes to further those purposes.

ORR's proactive inspections and reactive investigations (which relate to all of the relevant statutory provisions) are carried out under this. ORR has a similar duty, articulated in the Safety Directive, to monitor and supervise the compliance of railway undertakings and infrastructure managers with national and European law.

### Health and safety permissions and approvals

The ORR grants health and safety permissions and approvals to railway operators. There is detailed guidance on how to apply. These are the main areas where a legal approval may be needed from the ORR:

- Entities in charge of maintenance certification;
- Interoperability authorisations;
- Level crossings;
- Private Acts and Orders consents and approvals;
- Rail vehicle accessibility;

- Railway safety regulations exemptions;
- Safety certificates, authorisations and exemptions;
- Train driver licensing;

These are explained below.

## Enforcement

The ORR has the duty to make adequate arrangements for the enforcement of HSWA and the relevant statutory provisions

**Sections 21 and 22 of the HSWA** describe the powers of inspectors to serve improvement and prohibition enforcement notices. Section 33 describes the offences under the HSWA. These powers relate to all enforcing authorities of the Health and Safety at Work Act.

The Health and Safety (Enforcing Authority for Railways and Other Guided Transport Systems) Regulations 2006 (EARR) set out the enforcement responsibilities of ORR. EARR was amended in 2008 to improve clarity in the division of enforcement responsibility. Activities or premises not allocated to ORR for enforcement under EARR Activities are subject to enforcement by either the Health and Safety Executive (HSE) or Local Authorities according to the Health and Safety (Enforcing Authority) Regulations 1998 (EA98).

### Making regulations

The ORR is:

- to submit such proposals as the ORR considers appropriate for the making of regulations for the railway safety purposes to the authorities having power to make regulations for those purposes under any of the relevant statutory provisions.

## Other functions (under Section 1 HSWA/RAOS)

- to make such arrangements as ORR considers appropriate for the carrying out of research in connection with the railway safety purposes and for the publication of the results of such research
- to encourage research by others in that connection
- to make such arrangements as ORR considers appropriate for the provision of training and information in connection with the railway safety purposes

- to encourage the provision by others of training and information in that connection and
- to make such arrangements as ORR considers appropriate for providing an information and advisory service with respect to matters relevant to the railway safety purposes to government departments, employers, employees and certain others

## Railways and other Guided Transport Systems (Safety) Regulations 2006 (ROGS)

The rail industry must comply with the requirements of the ROGS. One of ORR's primary roles is to check that the railway operators have, and implemented, an effective health and safety management system that protects workers, passengers and others from harm, so far as is reasonably practicable. ORR's main role under these regulations is to assess safety management systems of TOCs and Infrastructure managers and, if satisfied, issue safety certificates or authorisations. After certification, ORR monitors compliance with the regime as above.

## The Railways (Accident Investigation and Reporting) Regulations 2005

Recommendations made by RAIB following an investigation must be addressed to ORR and ORR must consider them and, if necessary, take steps to ensure they are implemented.

## The Level Crossings Act 1983

The Act authorises the Secretary of State for Transport to make level crossing orders for the protection of those using a level crossing while taking account of both safety and convenience aspects of crossings. The order can specify the protection arrangements required at certain types of crossing. This function is usually performed by the ORR on behalf of the Secretary of State. Level crossing orders cover individual level crossings.

*Related non-safety legislation*

## Railways (Interoperability) Regulations 2006 (RIR 2006)

ORR has a duty under these regulations to authorise new vehicles and infrastructure that fall within the scope of those regulations. This requires ORR to assess the technical file created in relation to the project and certify that the project meets the 'essential requirements'. Train Driving Licences and Certificates Regulations 2010.

Under EU requirements (Directive 2014/82), any new driver must have a train driver licence and certificate to drive on the mainline railway. Existing drivers will need both by 29 October 2018. ORR is the authority tasked with issuing train driving licences. ORR also has a duty under these regulations to maintain a register of professionals capable of assessing fitness to drive trains (doctors/psychologists etc.). Doctors, psychometric assessors and training and examination centres who assess new train drivers must be recognised by ORR.

Rail Vehicle Accessibility (Non-Interoperable Rail System) Regulations 2010

ORR is the enforcing authority for these regulations which set out accessibility standards for the construction of rail vehicles not subject to RIR 2006 – i.e. the accessibility standards to which new non-mainline (and older rail vehicles as and when they are refurbished) must comply.

European Directive Requirements

There are a number of requirements in European Directives (notably the Safety Directive) which have not been transposed into UK law and yet are binding on ORR as the UK Safety Authority. These include items such as producing the annual safety report and checking compliance with the requirements for entities in charge of maintenance.

Exemptions

In addition to the above ORR has the power to grant exemptions from a number of the requirements of regulations enforced by it (such as ROGS and the Rail Safety Regulations 1999).

*Conflicting functions and duties*

There is likely to be an even stronger need for accountability and transparency in decision making and reporting if there are conflicts, or perceived conflicts, between objectives, roles, duties or functions of a particular regulator

The ORR has not identified any direct conflicts between functions, but has noted the potential conflicts between the duties that ORR follows in exercising its functions. For instance, in determining track access decisions ORR needs to balance its duty to promote competition with the need to have regard to the funds available to the Secretary of State, as the granting of new access rights can extract expected franchise income from the government.

UK policy makers take the view that managing potential conflicts requires a body independent of government and other stakeholders to balance the complex interests of various stakeholders (e.g. funders and users) to ensure decisions are made without regard to short-term political considerations (see below regarding the ORR Board). Ultimately where there is conflict it is the application of the Board's expert judgment in making trade-offs for the long-term benefit of users and funders that is applied.

*Organisation*

As noted in the introduction, independence is an important ingredient to ensuring longer term perspectives and commitment in regulatory decision making. In the case of the ORR, there is a clear decision making process that is based on the attributes of good regulation: evidence-based, open, transparent, principled and consultative.

The decision makers are entitled to use their judgement to make the appropriate trade-offs in accordance with the relevant facts and appropriate duties relating to function in question. The importance of making these decisions in a clear, transparent manner becomes essential for the long term support of the regulator and acceptance of its decisions.

In that regard, the ORR Board is comprised of full-time executive directors and part-time non-executive directors. The majority of directors are non-executive with a variety of backgrounds to provide broad experience in approaching the complex and varied decisions that must be taken. The Board is independent of all other parties and is responsible for:

- setting strategic direction;
- appointing and removing the chief executive;
- monitoring performance and ensuring ORR's legal obligations are met.

The Board has overall legal responsibility for all the activities of the ORR.

While executive directors are professional experts in their fields (economic and/or safety regulation) the non-executive directors are appointed from various backgrounds with commercial, technical, legal, administrative and/or economic expertise. While legislation does not specify the set of skills and experience required of Board members, candidates are selected according to the well-established public appointment rules of the Civil Service. Appointments to the Board are formally made by the secretary of state following the selection process for a fixed period and, once appointed, all Board members are required to act independently.

Executive directors are appointed for terms in line with civil service contracts of employment, while non-executive directors are typically appointed for four year terms.

### Reform agenda

There have been no major reforms undertaken in the last five years, although as noted above some additional responsibilities have been added to the ORR. As noted above, following the Infrastructure Act 2015 the ORR took on new responsibilities for overseeing the performance of Highways England, which is the government-owned company that runs the strategic highways network in England. This brings the oversight of the highways sector onto a more independent footing, which reflects elements of the arrangements for rail. Following a change to EU legislation, the ORR is also adopting responsibility for overseeing access and charges for the Channel Tunnel. The ORR will execute this function jointly with the French rail regulator, *Autorité de Régulation des Activités Ferroviaires* (ARAF). The ORR will also become the rail regulator in Northern Ireland following the implementation of Directive 2012/34 establishing a single European railway area.

## Accountability and transparency

As noted previously, a regulator that aspires to world class status needs a comprehensive set of measures by which it may be judged and measured and that reflect its objectives, duties and functions. The legislature, relevant departments, regulated businesses and the general public need to be able to not only assess the regulator's efficiency in carrying out its mandate but also its effectiveness. The regulator also requires measures by which it can effectively assess itself in order to improve and meet the needs of evolving markets and expectations.

There are, as noted previously, different types of accountability. The formal type, where the entity is going to be held accountable to the political body that provides oversight (Parliament, government, various committees of the Parliament); accountable to the courts through judicial review proceedings; and the more informal type, that is a more general accountability relating all stakeholders and not necessarily underpinned by legislative arrangements.

## Accountability to a minister and legislature

Formally, the ORR is accountable solely to the Parliament. While members of the Board are appointed by the Minister they are not accountable to him/her but, as noted above, they are appointed to be independent of Ministerial control. The Minister is unable to direct the regulator or to overrule regulatory decisions. While the Minister may provide "guidance" to the ORR about the exercise of its functions, this is rarely done and always done publicly through a published letter. However while the Secretary of State can provide guidance and make representations, he cannot direct the Board.

While the ORR does not have a written statement of expectations its functions, duties and powers are clearly stated in its enabling legislation. These are readily accessible via the ORR's website, which provides a significant amount of information. The website has a clear articulation of ORR's functions under various headings, beginning with a simple statement as to its role ("ORR regulate the rail industry's health and safety performance and ORR holds Network Rail and High Speed 1 (HS1) to account and the ORR make sure the rail industry is competitive and fair").

The website also lists the ORR's set of functions and identifies the role under each of these:

- ORR and safety – providing guidance, conducting research, publishing reports, inspections, investigations and enforcement action.

- ORR and Network Rail – setting strategic direction for NR, monitoring delivery against targets, publish reports, scrutinises NR's performance and investment

- ORR and HS1- validate performance and efficiency targets, monitor performance and efficiency, and publish reports.

- ORR: fair access and fair treatment – license train operators, stations, maintenance and networks, approve access arrangements, and investigate competition issues and provide consumer protection.

- ORR and customers – ensure reliable information, report on performance for public, investigate complaints, carry out research and publish reports, ensure passenger engagement in project developments, hold NR to account for reliable and timely services.

As noted previously, the ORR provides a clear, simple statement of its duties without requiring an observer to navigate through dense pieces of legislation and Parliamentary Acts.

*Annual Business Plans*

Along with the ORR's formal accountability to Parliament, there are several measures in place to ensure that this accountability is tested. Firstly, the ORR publishes an annual business plan which provides the reader with its strategic objectives (see page 3 of this case study) and provides a number of measures, both quantitative and qualitative around those measures. The business plan identifies medium and long term outcomes under each of its strategic objectives. The plan then notes a number of activities taken from its 2014-15 work programs that are expected to contribute to achieving the longer term outcomes specified in the plan.

This is a strong accountability mechanism that commits the ORR to achieving and reporting on a number of goals that, taken together, provide a good picture of the operational success or otherwise of the regulator.

For example, under its Drive for Safety strategic objective, the ORR commits to longer term outcomes around continuous improvement, demonstrating a healthy and safe environment that are driven by the industry with less involvement by ORR. To support these longer term outcomes the ORR identifies quantitative and qualitative indicators such as:

- Duty holders are seen to implement excellent health and safety management systems;
- A 50% reduction in catastrophic train accident risk;
- No less than 25% reduction in risk at level crossings;
- A significant reduction in worker safety risk from improvements in Road Rail Vehicles and improvement in protection of track workers for example;
- An improvement in the management of, and consequent reduction in, passenger-train interface risk; and
- An improvement by the industry in the measurement and management of occupational health.

The Business Plan then outlines a series of activities that will be undertaken to achieve the outcomes identified under the headings of:

- Enforcing the law;
- Ensuring risk is managed effectively; and
- Driving continual improvement.

Each of the ORR's five strategic objectives has a similar set of long-term and medium-term outcomes with a set of activities for the coming year that are meant to achieve these outcomes. The ORR intends to apply this approach to an additional sixth objective that relates to its new roads functions.

*Annual Report and Audit*

Along with the business plan, the ORR has a requirement, enforced by the statutory auditor, the National Audit Office (NAO), to publish an Annual Report. The Annual Report[11] summarises the key activities and events of the reporting year against the framework of the objectives set out in the business plan. This is a key tool in terms of both accountability and transparency, as it provides substantial performance information in a format that is easy to understand and assess.

The Annual Report provides the usual audited financial report that provides confidence to the Parliament that ORR is adhering to appropriate financial standards. In addition the report takes the strategic objectives from the Business Plan and considers each one in light of what has been accomplished over the year.

For example, under the heading of Drive for a safer railway (Strategic Objective 1) the ORR lists a number of areas identified for improvement and then notes that actions taken over the year to address them. Under Level crossing risks the report states that "Network Rail has achieved a 30.9% reduction in risk, mostly through closure of level crossings – this exceeds the 25% target…"

The full set of areas identified includes the following with each area having a commentary around actions taken and where possible quantification of those actions:

- Signals passed at danger;
- Protecting the safety of passengers;
- Track worker safety;
- Track twist faults;
- Occupational health;
- Transport for London's Underground;
- Heritage railways.

*Publication of Decisions*

While the ORR has an internal requirement to publish all major decisions, there are also statutory and legal requirements to publish certain types of decisions and give reasons. Under RA93, ORR must maintain a public register of all decisions relating to licences, access agreements, exemptions, consents and enforcement action in respect of its rail economic functions. On the safety side, under the Environment and Safety Act 1988 we publish details of all improvement and prohibition enforcement notices served on business and prosecutions are a matter of public record. Publishing decisions is a good practice in terms of providing stakeholders with an understanding of the reasons behind decisions. It helps maintain confidence in the regulator that it is adhering to analytical rigour and evidence–based assessments in its decision making.

*Parliamentary Committees*

As in many regulatory regimes, the ORR is required to participate as a witness and answer questions or provide evidence to Parliamentary Committees. These committees, the Transport Select Committees and the Public Accounts Committee, scrutinise the ORR's work performance in their roles overseeing government policy and performance.

*Key Performance Indicators*

Developing appropriate and relevant Key Performance Indicators (KPIS) that allow for meaningful assessment of regulatory performance has been a major challenge for regulators across the globe for a number of years. The ORR observes that this is a complex and difficult area due in large part to:

- A significant aspect of the regulator's work being to ensure the prevention of harm, which by its very nature is difficult to measure;

- The difficulty in attributing responsibility for outcomes in dynamic, open markets.

The ORR only commits to specific performance indicators where it is able to do so with a clear line of sight and responsibility. It does, however, track a wide range of data that enables judgements as to market and industry developments and to adjust settings accordingly. Importantly, it also undertakes *ex ante* and *ex post* assessments of significant regulatory decisions and policies, which while accepting the difficulty of determining causality noted above, also details these where necessary so an observer will understand and appreciate the issues.

The ORR does publish its outcomes, although this is not subject to any agreement from Ministers or the Parliament.

## *Accountability to regulated entities*

Different aspects of the ORR's regulatory decisions may attract different appeals mechanisms. For example, the Competition Appeals Tribunal (e.g. for competition cases) or to the CMA (e.g. for the periodic review of network infrastructure). In respect of access decisions, it is open to either party to challenge an ORR determination by way of judicial review proceedings in the High Court.

These paths and associated processes are well understood and the mechanisms for the different aspects of regulation are detailed on the ORR website. These bodies are all independent of the regulator. There are clearly defined processes set out by the appeals bodies and the decisions are binding on all parties. There is no formal internal review unit established in the ORR.

The broad suite of information that it provides on its performance clearly allows regulated entities to make judgements as to the ORR's approach to regulation and to assess whether or not and to what level it has achieved the targets it has set. It also, in the first instance, allows businesses to determine if they believe these targets are appropriate measures of performance.

Evaluations, whether *ex post* or *ex ante*, are also important measures in building high accountability standards in regard to the regulated businesses, as well as providing the ORR with a check on their regulatory decisions and the cost-benefit impact of those decisions. As with many measure, there is a dual management and outward accountability benefit. The ORR has committed to conduct and publish impact assessments in a greater number of areas, allowing external parties to assess the reasonableness and impact of decisions.

## *Accountability to the public*

Many of the processes and publications noted above in the accountability sections are relevant to the public as well. The publication of reports, decisions, business plans etc. accessible to the public is evidence of a transparent approach to the provision of relevant information. Public accountability, which by definition is not necessarily targeting the informed expert, needs to have measures that are understandable. That is, both accessible and assessable so that just being able to find the information may not be sufficient. It also needs to be in a format that can be understood and interpreted by interested parties.

In addition to the measures identified the ORR routinely commissions an independent review of its 5-yearly periodic review of the network infrastructure. This recognises the particular significance of this particular legislation. It also notes that the NAO is able to, and does, initiate and publish its own reviews into various aspects of the ORR's work. It also annually reviews the operational efficiency of the ORR on behalf of Parliament.

All regulatory policies are published while operational policies are disclosable under Freedom of Information (FOI) laws. The ORR has a well-developed web site rich in information and with easily accessed links to all aspects of its work.

## Transparency

Given the range of its responsibilities, the ORR has a substantial commitment to accountability through transparent information provision, public engagement, data provision, consultation and *ex ante* and post assessment.

Many of the measures discussed above are of relevance to the ORR's commitment to transparency. While the ORR has a legal guarantee of independence, its behaviour in exercising its functions and the openness with which it undertakes and reports on these functions is extremely important.

In the introduction section on accountability and transparency, formal accountability through Parliament and the Courts was identified as an important and fundamental aspect of the safeguards that ensure independence is not abused. Likewise, transparency in operations, decision making, guidance and other policies is an important aspect underpinning the credibility, integrity and continued acceptance of an independent ORR.

The FOI laws that the ORR is subject to provide another level of transparency, although they do not inform the regulator as to what information it needs to provide in the first instance. However, it is embedded in the regular practice of the ORR that it consults widely on its policies and undertakes rigorous evidence-based impact assessments. These processes are subject to a proportionality test to provide some assurance that stakeholders are not over-burdened or incur unnecessary costs in engaging with the regulator.

Considering the strength of the FOI laws in supporting transparency, the ORR notes that the procedures and protections around confidentiality of information and limits to access are well established and explained.

In regards to performance information, this note has already identified that there is a variety of means for disseminating these to the public:

- The business plan and annual report are both published and provide reports against performance.
- *Ex ante* and *ex post* impact assessments are conducted for significant aspects of regulation.
- A range of market information and statistics are gathered and published routinely to measure market developments and to inform interested parties in the development of regulatory policy and to assess the success of policies to date.
- The ORR also publishes a range of performance data relating to the industries it regulates including: quarterly data reports, a six-monthly monitor of Network Rail's performance against regulatory outputs; annual efficiency review of Network Rail; annual report of finances and funding of the rail industry; statistics about rail usage, safety and funding; and ad hoc market studies into various aspects of the rail sector.

There is another aspect to accountability and transparency that is extremely important for regulators. That is, making sure that consumers of particular services are well informed in terms of their decisions as to the services they actually consume. That is, empowered and informed customers. The ORR includes public authorities that provide funding as part of this segment.

To this end it looks to the provision of quality, trusted information on performance of the sector, costs and funding as fundamental to enabling customers to understand and therefore make judgements on the manner in which fares are set and tax payer funds are used.

Transparency in the form of these information flows should ensure the markets work better and deliver what consumers and customers want, not what the industry players believe they want. This ensures that choices are available and that the public using rail is aware of these and the appropriate trade-offs. This greatly supports consumer choice and demonstrates that accountability and transparency through the provisions of information is not just about determining the effectiveness or efficiency in more narrow terms.

## Concluding insights

The ORR has a strong commitment to accountability in both the formal sense (to Parliament and the Courts) and informally to the many stakeholders that take a direct and indirect interest in its regulatory decisions. There are a range of measures that have been put in place to provide all stakeholders with a basis for the assessment of the effectiveness of the regulator in carrying out its mandates.

Given that these measures are open and transparent they are highly likely to provide strong incentives to the ORR to aim for and to maintain high quality regulatory performance and to ensure it is an effective steward of public authority and resources.

Many, if not all, of the measures discussed are assessable and accessible to stakeholders, with the intention of providing substantial and useful information for all parties. There is also an obvious willingness and commitment to revisit objectives, targets and strategies to test their appropriateness where circumstances may change and to develop views as to whether or not they have been successful in achieving the goals that the ORR has set for itself.

The ORR also adopts the position that its role is to help and inform users and consumers in their understanding of the fares and services they are provided and to underpin the concept of consumer choice in the sector. It does so through making available the right types of information in order that those users can make those informed, market driven decisions.

As a package of measures the ORR has developed a strong and transparent accountability framework that should be a useful model for other agencies.

# Notes

1. The remit of the ORR will be extended to Northern Ireland in 2016 so that it cover all the functions of the regulatory body set out in Directive 2012/34/EU of the European Parliament and of the Council of 21 November 2012 establishing a single European railway area.

2. For example: The Railways Act 2005; the Railways Act 1993; the Railways and other Guided Transport Systems (Safety) Regulations 2006; the Rail Vehicle Accessibility Regulations 2010; Railways Infrastructure (Access and Management) Regulations 2005; Railway (Licensing of Railway Undertakings) Regulations 2005; and the Health and Safety at Work Act 1974.

3. http://orr.gov.uk/about-orr/what-we-do; includes links to the laws, duties and functions of ORR.

4. http://orr.gov.uk/what-and-how-we-regulate/regulation-of-network-rail.http://orr.gov.uk/what-and-how-we-regulate/regulation-of-network-railhttp://orr.gov.uk/what-and-how-we-regulate/regulation-of-network-rail

5. http://orr.gov.uk/what-and-how-we-regulate/track-accesshttp://orr.gov.uk/what-and-how-we-regulate/track-access.

6. http://orr.gov.uk/what-and-how-we-regulate/station-and-depot-accesshttp://orr.gov.uk/what-and-how-we-regulate/station-and-depot-access.

7. http://orr.gov.uk/what-and-how-we-regulate/licensing.

8. http://orr.gov.uk/what-and-how-we-regulate/competition-and-consumershttp://orr.gov.uk/what-and-how-we-regulate/competition-and-consumers.

9. http://orr.gov.uk/what-and-how-we-regulate/investmentshttp://orr.gov.uk/what-and-how-we-regulate/investments.

10. http://orr.gov.uk/what-and-how-we-regulate/competition-and-consumers/market-studies. http://orr.gov.uk/what-and-how-we-regulate/competition-and-consumers/market-studies

11. See http://orr.gov.uk/.

# Bibliography

ORR (2015a), "Business Plan 2015-16", March, http://orr.gov.uk/__data/assets/pdf_file/0018/17622/business-plan-2015-16.pdf (accessed 24 July 2015).

ORR (2015b), "Annual Report and Accounts 2014-15", http://orr.gov.uk/__data/assets/pdf_file/0019/18154/annual-report-2014-15-web.pdf (accessed 24 July 2015).

## Chapter 6

## Mexico's key sector and regulatory reforms

*This chapter presents some of the key reforms introduced by Mexico in relation to energy, telecommunications and competition and some of the related changes in the governance of regulators.*

In 2013, Mexico introduced a comprehensive package of structural reforms aimed at increasing productivity, strengthen and extend rights and improve democratic institutions. The governance of regulators has been an important component of these reforms, which have established autonomous regulatory institutions whose independence is guaranteed by the Constitution. These institutions have replaced ministerial regulators and semi-autonomous agencies in key sectors of the economy. The following sections provide an overview of some the reforms in the energy and telecommunication sectors as well as in the area of economic competition.[1]

## Energy

The 2013 reform introduced a transformation concerning the Mexican oil industry and set forth the activities regarding the National Electric System. It aims at having a larger availability of oil, natural gas and its derivatives, as well as an electricity service of better quality and greater coverage at competitive rates by modernising the energy sector in Mexico.

Regarding oil activities, the reform opens the sector to competition in order to attract investment. The Mexican Oil Company (PEMEX) was granted a new governance structure, as well as technical and management autonomy. The National Electric System has been opened up to the participation of electricity-generating companies in order to reduce electricity costs and develop the transition to renewable sources of energy as well as extending electricity coverage.

In August 2014, President Enrique Peña Nieto enacted the secondary legislation of the energy reform, composed of 9 new initiatives and amendments to 12 existing ones as well as an Implementation Decalogue.[2] The package of secondary laws provides for the creation of several regulatory entities, including the National Energy Control Centre (CENACE), the National Centre for Control of Natural Gas (CENAGAS), the National Centre for Hydrocarbon Information (CNIH) and the Agency of Industrial Safety and Environmental Protection in the Oil and Gas Sector (ASEA). The reform also strengthened existing regulators such as the National Hydrocarbon Commission (CNH) and the Energy Regulation

1. The reforms also includes actions aimed at improving financial markets, labour policies, taxation, education, justice, the political and electoral process and transparency.

2. Valenzuela and Wood (2014), "Mexico's Energy Reform: entering the final phase – The Expert Take", Wilson Centre, http://wilsoncenter.org/article/mexico%E2%80%99s-energy-reform-entering-the-final-phase-the-expert-take (accessed 24 July 2015).

Commission (CRE). CENACE and CENAGAS are in charge of regulating the electricity and gas markets, taking over some of the regulatory functions of the Federal Energy Commission (CFE) and PEMEX (Figure 6.1).

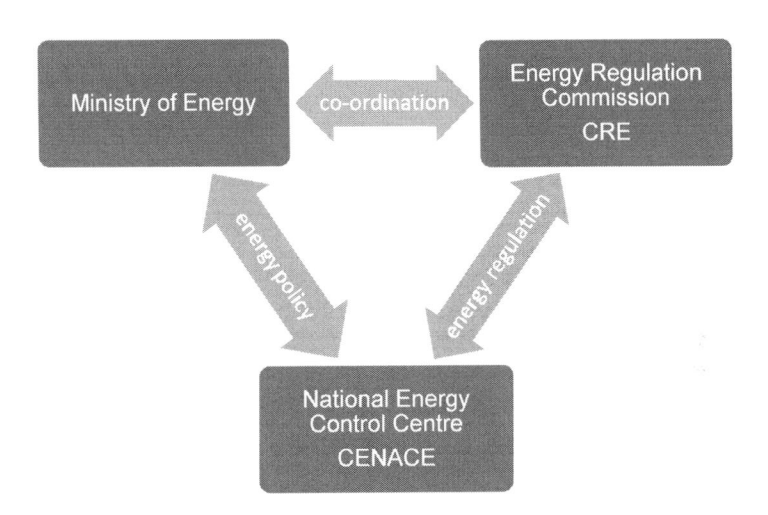

Figure 6.1. **Energy regulatory framework in Mexico**

```
       Ministry of Energy  <--co-ordination-->  Energy Regulation
                                                 Commission
                                                    CRE
                    \ energy policy      energy regulation /
                            National Energy
                            Control Centre
                                CENACE
```

*Source*: CENACE presentation at the Mexico Energy Forum, 11 Feb 2015.

## *The governance of the energy regulators*

These reforms provide a real-case example of the close interdependence between governance arrangements. The CRE was granted its own legal personality, greater powers and responsibilities, technical and management autonomy, and an autonomous source of funding (beside the national budget) through fees for the issuance and management of permissions, authorisations, assignments, contracts, and services related to the national information centre of hydrocarbons.

Rules for board appointment and dismissal have also changed. The Board of CRE has been expanded to seven members, and the mandate of the commissioners has been extended to seven years, with fixed dates for mandates' start and end. The Senate appoints Board members on the basis of proposals made by the President. Commissioners need to have a minimum of five years of experience in the sector and at least one year of no ties with the regulated entities previous to the appointment. Under the new legislation, dismissal can only occur through a process that involves the

Senate and the executive branch and only for the violations identified in the Coordinated Energy Regulatory Agencies Act.

Greater independence from the executive and more extensive powers and responsibilities have been accompanied by an effort towards enhanced accountability and transparency. The CRE collects and publishes more performance information and has also established an Evaluation Committee, chaired by CRE Chairman and composed of relevant CRE directors, to evaluate the effectiveness of the regulatory policy implemented by the CRE. Proposals for new regulations must be submitted to the Federal Commission for Regulatory Improvement (COFEMER), which is responsible for promoting regulatory quality.

In addition, the reforms have created the need for well-functioning co-ordination mechanisms between the executive and the independent regulatory agencies, which have now become autonomous actors in the policy-making process. The Law of Coordinated Regulators, (*Ley de Órganos Reguladores Coordinados en materia energética*) establishes the functions and duties of both CNH and CRE. It also states that they will have to co-ordinate with the Ministry of Energy in order for its decisions to be coherent with the national energy policies. The CNH grants contracts to private actors for exploration and exploitation of oil and gas, while CRE grants permits to private companies interested in generating and supplying electricity. An Energy Sector Co-ordination Council brings together ministerial departments and regulators to help align the work programmes of the regulators with the objectives of the government's energy policy and make recommendations on actions to facilitate the implementation of the energy policy.

## Telecommunications

The telecommunications reform has two main objectives:

- Integrating Mexico into the knowledge society by fostering a policy of universal digital inclusion that seeks to increase access of citizens to information and communication technologies;

- Fostering competition regarding telecommunication services in order for final users to have more options and better prices.

The reform aims at attracting investment in sectors like satellite communications and radio broadcasting. The Mexican government expects that the reform will impact positively on growth and productivity; as well as aid in strengthening democracy; and, foster universal access to culture and education. Some of the relevant objectives are the following:

- *Update of the normative framework.* A law that regulates the use of the radio broadcasting spectrum, the networks and telecommunications services, was enacted. It establishes a unique concession regime for the delivery of services and asymmetric regulatory measures.

- *Strengthening the institutional framework.* The Federal Telecommunications Institute (IFT) was created as an autonomous body in charge of the regulation, promotion and supervision of the radio wavelength spectrum, the networks and the delivery of telecommunications and radio services. It also functions as an economic competition authority in that sector.

- *Promote competition.* The IFT has tools to reduce levels of concentration and foster competition. Foreign investment is permitted in telecommunications and satellite communication up to 100%.

## Economic competition

The Federal Economic Competition Law's objective is to boost a more competitive, just and transparent market. The Mexican government updated the normative framework and strengthened the regulator in charge of the sector. The catalogue of anticompetitive practices was expanded and sanctions increased in order to protect consumer's rights.

The reform has three strategic objectives:

- *New institutional design.* It creates the Federal Economic Competition Commission (COFECE) as a body of the Mexican State. It provides for mechanisms that guarantee independent, professional, technical and impartial decisions. It sets out mechanisms of control, accountability and transparency for the regulator as well as it assigns an internal comptroller to review the acts of the COFECE officials.

- *Broaden the anticompetitive practices catalogue.* It further defines what should be understood as an anticompetitive practice and the sanctions available for such acts. It also prohibits monopolies and monopolistic practices.

- *A higher quality legislative instrument.* Provides for a defined, clear and certain application of the law by defining the due process and the rights of the economic agents. Furthermore it strengthens the ability of COFECE to sanction anticompetitive practices.

## Bibliography

Valenzuela P. and Wood D. (2014), "Mexico's Energy Reform: Entering the Final Phase – The Expert Take", Wilson Centre, http://wilsoncenter.org/article/mexico%E2%80%99s-energy-reform-entering-the-final-phase-the-expert-take (accessed 24 July 2015).

# ORGANISATION FOR ECONOMIC CO-OPERATION AND DEVELOPMENT

The OECD is a unique forum where governments work together to address the economic, social and environmental challenges of globalisation. The OECD is also at the forefront of efforts to understand and to help governments respond to new developments and concerns, such as corporate governance, the information economy and the challenges of an ageing population. The Organisation provides a setting where governments can compare policy experiences, seek answers to common problems, identify good practice and work to co-ordinate domestic and international policies.

The OECD member countries are: Australia, Austria, Belgium, Canada, Chile, the Czech Republic, Denmark, Estonia, Finland, France, Germany, Greece, Hungary, Iceland, Ireland, Israel, Italy, Japan, Korea, Luxembourg, Mexico, the Netherlands, New Zealand, Norway, Poland, Portugal, the Slovak Republic, Slovenia, Spain, Sweden, Switzerland, Turkey, the United Kingdom and the United States. The European Union takes part in the work of the OECD.

OECD Publishing disseminates widely the results of the Organisation's statistics gathering and research on economic, social and environmental issues, as well as the conventions, guidelines and standards agreed by its members.